Copyright © 2017

Published by Lifewater International
P.O. Box 3131
San Luis Obispo, CA 93403
www.lifewater.org

Designed by: Rule29 Creative
www.rule29.com

Printed by: O'Neil Printing
www.oneilprint.com

Unless otherwise indicated, Scripture is taken from the THE HOLY BIBLE, NEW INTERNATIONAL VERSION®, NIV® Copyright © 1973, 1978, 1984, 2011 by Biblica, Inc.® Used by permission. All rights reserved worldwide. Quotation marked NRSV is taken from the New Revised Standard Version Bible, copyright © 1989 the Division of Christian Education of the National Council of the Churches of Christ in the United States of America. Used by permission. All rights reserved.

All rights reserved. No part of this book may be reproduced in any form or by any means electric or mechanical, including photocopying, recording, or by any information storage and retrieval system, without permission in writing from the author.

ISBN 978-0-692-84607-0

Printed in the United States of America

Though Your Footprints Were Not Seen

I will remember the deeds of the Lord;
yes, I will remember your miracles of long ago.
I will consider all your works
and meditate on all your mighty deeds
Your ways, God, are holy.
What god is as great as our God?
You are the God who performs miracles;
you display your power among the peoples.
With your mighty arm you redeemed your people,
the descendants of Jacob and Joseph.
The waters saw you, God,
the waters saw you and writhed;
the very depths were convulsed
The clouds poured down water,
the heavens resounded with thunder;
your arrows flashed back and forth.
Your thunder was heard in the whirlwind,
your lightning lit up the world;
the earth trembled and quaked.
Your path led through the sea,
your way through the mighty waters,
though your footprints were not seen.

Psalm 77:11-19

DEDICATION

To Lorraine,

"A wife of noble character who can find? She is worth far more than rubies" (Proverbs 31:10). I did. She is far more precious than jewels.

To my four children, fourteen grandchildren and eighteen great-grandchildren,

I am so grateful for my loving family who God provided that will "tell the next generation the praiseworthy deeds of the LORD, his power, and the wonders he has done" (Psalm 78:4). May you always "seek first his kingdom and his righteousness" (Matthew 6:33) for the fulfillment He provides.

To the myriad of friends who've offered love, support, and encouragement—especially the Lifewater board, staff and volunteers who have been my coworkers. You have shown me that "in Christ we, though many, form one body, and each member belongs to all the others" (Romans 12:5).

Thank you all.

CONTENTS

PREFACE 1

PART I   *The Life That Led Me to Lifewater*
Chapter 1   Nature and Nurture 5
Chapter 2   Companions for Life 13

PART II   *A Ministry of Word and Deed*
Chapter 3   Seeds of a Ministry 25
Chapter 4   The Birth of Lifewater 37
Chapter 5   Our Early Years 47

PART III   *Lifewater Goes Global*
Chapter 6   The Dominican Republic: The Hand Pump 61
Chapter 7   Kenya: Our First Shop 65
Chapter 8   Haiti: My Last Trip 67
Chapter 9   Return to Kenya: A Student Named Paul 71
Chapter 10   Nigeria: Soap and Water 79
Chapter 11   North Africa: Gaining Access to a Closed Country .. 87
Chapter 12   Philippines: "The Babies Don't Die Anymore" 97
Chapter 13   Romania: Pollution Control 105
Chapter 14   Sudan: Where Women Led the Charge 117
Chapter 15   Tanzania: The Most Likely of Places to Start 121
Chapter 16   Uganda: The Ravages of War 129
Chapter 17   Uzbekistan: The Poisonous Aral Sea 135
Chapter 18   Zambia: Where Women Bear the Water 137
Chapter 19   Zimbabwe: Solar Oven and Water Strategy 145

PART IV — *Lifewater Innovations and Strategies*

Chapter 20	Short-Term Workers	151
Chapter 21	Short-Term Worker Conferences	155
Chapter 22	The Bush Pump	159
Chapter 23	Pump Repair Ministry	161

CONCLUSION 163

APPENDIX

Lifewater Friends and Partners 167
Friends Who Influenced My Life 171

PREFACE

The life of every Christian has a divinely ordained purpose, including mine. Many friends have challenged me to write Lifewater's story, which is in many ways inextricably bound with my own. These pages record my determination to "press on toward the goal to win the prize for which God has called me heavenward in Christ Jesus" (Philippians 3:14). In this respect, it is *my* story.

But I am very clear that what I am sharing is also a privileged glimpse of God's story. Again and again I've recognized that so many events others might label as "coincidence" have been the work of God's gracious hand. The Scriptures confirm that God is not capricious. In fact, in the tenth chapter of Luke's Gospel Jesus teaches us, through the story of a gracious Samaritan, that unexpected events can be opportunities to serve others the way Jesus would. They are divine appointments to meet the needs of others in Jesus' name.

Over years and decades God has allowed me to witness His footprints unseen. God's "footprints" (Psalm 77:19) are spiritual paths we learn to discern and follow as we pay attention to the voice of the Holy Spirit in our souls, guiding us to take action. It is my delight to share some that have guided Lifewater's history.

My prayer has been that these words will challenge and help you.

To God be all glory,

William ("Bill") Ashe

"To this you were called, because Christ suffered for you, leaving you an example, that you should follow in his steps."
(1 Peter 2:21)

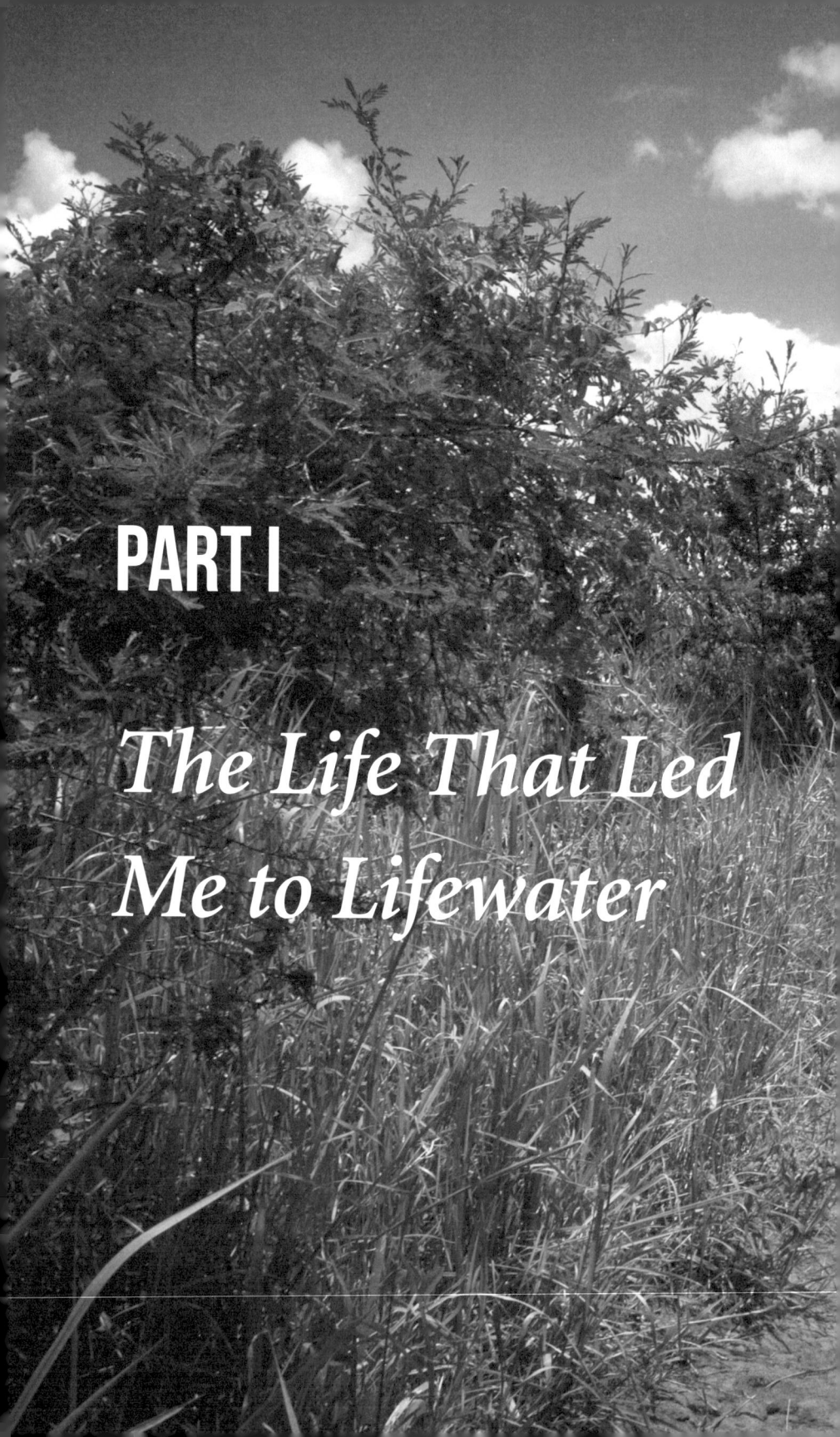

PART I

The Life That Led Me to Lifewater

CHAPTER 1
Nature and Nurture

My father's father, my great-grandfather Gregory G. Ashe, emigrated from Ireland's Kerry County to the United States in1848, at the age of twenty-two. As a young man he served with the flotilla of the United States Navy. When discharged he received a 160-acre land grant from the government, for his service, signed by President James Buchanan on May 1, 1860. The land was in White City, Kansas. Our family still has it.

My great-grandmother, with whom Greg raised four children, kept a diary of their life together that we also still have. She writes that when Greg went to Kansas City to get food staples she was frightened by "Indians outside the gate." It is unclear how many years went by before they built their home on the land they'd received.

My grandfather Fred was the youngest child. When I was growing up I often heard others refer to my grandparents, Fred and Molly, as "fine Christian folks." I was named after my Uncle Bill Ashe, a brother to my grandfather who was beloved by my father.

After their marriage, Fred and his wife, Molly, hardworking pioneers, moved to Tarkio, Missouri, in search of new opportunity. This is the town where my father and his three siblings, two brothers and a sister, grew up. Though the Depression had wiped out his family's assets, my father was working and bought a five-acre ranch in Riverside, California, for his parents and two brothers. I still have fond memories from my own childhood of our journeys from our home in Burbank to Riverside to spend weekends with my grandparents and uncles. Grandmother Molly made wonderful meals, including her famous apple pie. As a small boy, these weekends let this city boy taste farm life, wandering through their garden and playing with their chickens.

As I look back on my grandfather's life, I can see how God marked a trail of life through Fred's faithfulness that laid the groundwork of "footprints unseen" in my own life.

In1928, Fred was directing sales for Dempster Windmill Company. He died in 1933. In 1965, though, it "just so happened" that our family company, Shaw Pump and Supply, began selling Dempster windmills.

That connection, knitting me to my grandfather, has always been precious to me. And I count it an unmistakable divine appointment because the Dempster Windmill was the unlikely opportunity for my first mission experience in 1965 when I installed one for an orphanage in Mexico.

Today, when I look back at a family photo showing my grandfather holding me in his arms at his Riverside ranch, I imagine that he might have whispered a blessing in my ear dedicating me to the Lord. Whether or not that happened, I thank God for the ways our Christian lives were forever linked.

My mother began her journey on the East Coast. Elsa was the oldest child of Arnold and Giannina Martinelli. They lived in Hoboken, New Jersey. Her father was an accomplished jewelry maker, watch repairman, oil paint artist and musician. My mother had two younger brothers, Enzo and Tony. Tragically, her parents both died during the Spanish influenza epidemic of 1918 when she was 15 years old.

Arnold's brother Arthur, called "Marty," was living in California with his wife, Annie, and their son at the time. Their son was the same age as Enzo. So they received the three orphans into their home in California. Marty was working at Goldwyn-Mayer in the film industry, making a good salary, so they were able to shoulder some of the additional expense of raising three children. All three boys went to military school, which was expensive. I'm not sure where the money came from, but I suspect there was money from the jewelry business Marty had sold before moving the children to California. Though he stretched the funds as best he could, I also suspect he paid some of the children's bills from his own pocket.

THEY CALLED ME BILLY

As long as I can remember, my parents called me Billy.

When I was two my parents purchased a house in Burbank and moved from Reno Street in Hollywood, where they'd been renting. This Burbank home, the bargain of my father's life, was being sold by a distressed, bankrupt builder. As everyone tried to get their footing after the Depression, it helped our family to have an investment instead of renting.

My parents were committed to taking me to Sunday school at our church, a large congregation in Los Angeles, where my mother sang in the choir. My earliest memories were of going to the city in the Hupmobile, one of the earliest automobiles built in the early twentieth century. I was always forced to wear a little man's suit made of coarse wool. I often begged, "Don't make me wear those scratchy pants." They finally decided to let me wear my pajama bottoms underneath! Unfortunately, I didn't learn much at this Sunday school; I just played.

Eventually driving to Los Angeles for church became too time-consuming and costly. By the time I was seven, after my sister Janet was born, we began attending a local church in Burbank. Mother, who had a beautiful soprano voice and was blessed with perfect pitch, joined the choir at this new church. She also sang in a Burbank choral group that traveled around Los Angeles County giving concerts.

At home, I was cherished. My mother, a kindergarten teacher, taught me piano, art and Italian—the language she'd spoken in her childhood home. She created her own book to teach me Italian words from pictures she'd drawn. When I was eight, I got my first bike for Christmas: a blue "Flyer."

Throughout childhood I wrestled with low self-esteem. I was always the youngest and skinniest kid in the class. In second grade the teacher quizzed us by showing us words on flashcards. Instead of teaching us phonics, the prevailing opinion among educators at that time was to teach children to recognize the shape of a word as a "picture." So children would sit in a semicircle as the teacher held up the flashcards. The child who called out the word first received the flashcard and placed it under his or her chair. At the end of the exercise the child with the most cards was declared the winner. I never won. When the teacher divided us into learning groups, I noticed that no one in my group had ever been one of the winners. And although it was never articulated by the teacher, I figured out I was in the group of slow learners. The system taught me that I was not one of the best. Even recess was difficult. My classmates knew I wasn't athletically gifted, and I always seemed to be chosen last for kickball or other sports. Also, I was frequently absent due to illness. I think this absenteeism also made it difficult for me to keep up with my class, exacerbating my negative feelings about myself compared to others.

One day, at a table beside the playground, I was eating lunch next to a boy from a different class when I noticed one of his hands. His fingers were all webbed except his thumb. I didn't say anything and quickly looked away. But it made an indelible impression upon me. I reasoned I must be more fortunate than he was since all of my fingers that worked separately. That moment was one of the first times the Lord put compassion in my heart for another.

My dad made a concerted effort to spend time with me on our vacations and holidays. One day we were hiking in the mountains and came across the first rattlesnake I ever saw. Dad killed it with a stone, frightening to both of us. At our cabin on Big Bear Lake we also spent time fishing together.

With money I earned from my paper route, I saved the seventy-nine dollars I needed to buy the kit to construct a Wizzer bike. It was a pretty big price tag back then! Although I struggled with kickball, I was mechanically capable. So it didn't take me long to convert my foot-pedaled bicycle to one that was power-driven. I modified the exhaust with a large aluminum conical tailpiece that acted like a trumpet. One day, when I was zipping down Burbank Boulevard, a police officer stopped me.

He asked, "What is that big tailpiece doing? Is it just to make noise?"

I explained, "No, the shape helps carry away the exhaust faster so the engine runs better."

The officer could hardly keep a straight face as he let me go.

My junior high school years were frustrating. I was shy, and a mild case of acne didn't help. Though I still struggled with academic classes, I received A's in wood shop and metal shop classes, excelling in creative design and model construction that would serve me well during my adult years. I continued to lean more toward mechanical things and engineering.

I sang in the school glee club and enjoyed those students. I was able to be a bit more outgoing with them.

David De Havilland was a good friend in junior high. We were in the same art class. David was a good artist and had a part-time job at Walt Disney Studios in the animation department. He encouraged me to also get a job there, but I never did. Later in life I took up oil painting and developed the artistic skills that were passed down from my mother's side of the family. Both my Grandfather Martinelli, who I'd never met, and my mother had been skilled artists. Though I enjoyed painting, my work never matched their quality.

At fourteen I got a Junior Operators Driver's License. A California law had dropped the eligible driving age to fourteen during World War II when eligible men drivers were scarce. At the DMV I passed the written test, missing only a few questions, and I passed my driving test with flying colors. When I handed my documents through the window to the examiner, he glanced down at my signature: "Billy Ashe."

Looking up at me he said, "When are you going to be 'Bill'?"

No one had ever asked me that before. His question, though, implied it was time. Maybe past time. So in that moment I decided. "Starting now."

HIGH SCHOOL YEARS

During high school I had a few girlfriends. Pat Hockensmith was a friend of Frances Reynolds, who we called Franny. So my friend Dick McCrane and I double-dated with both girls. When Franny won the Miss Burbank contest, the Warner Brothers Studio gave her a movie contract and changed her name to Debbie Reynolds.

During my teen years I joined a fellowship of young men called the Laurels. We had special maroon jackets with a patch on the back, and we were known in school as semi-bad boys. I recognize now that we were young men seeking purpose in life but too scared to admit it to each other.

Despite our largely unfounded reputation, the compassion that blossomed at a playground lunch table beside a boy with a physical difference began to develop in my teen years. Other people's misfortune, which would cause other boys to laugh, grieved me.

One day an overweight Billy Keyes, with a reputation for being a "sissy," arrived at school on his bicycle. Billy, being raised by his grandmother, always seemed to me like a kind, gentle guy. When he passed several of us in front of the parking lot, the boys with me began to laugh and jeer at him. Though I didn't speak up in that moment, my heart hurt for him. The following day in school, his grandmother announced that he'd swallowed rat poison and died.

I was crushed.

But the Holy Spirit used that event to teach me to have compassion for those who are rejected. It also triggered me to ask, "Where am I going? Why am I here on this earth? What am I going to do in life to support myself?"

They were all questions that the Lord would answer in His timing.

When I was fifteen my mother, the gifted soprano and concert pianist, tried to help me find a musical skill. She was convinced I'd received some of these genes. When I turned sixteen, my parents bought me a beautiful eighty-year-old double bass that I treasured. Because she wanted me to have the best training, Mother enlisted a professional Russian musician, Paul F. Gregory, who played with the Los Angeles Philharmonic Orchestra. Every Thursday afternoon we drove to Hollywood for my lesson. As my skills developed I joined the North Hollywood Junior Symphony orchestra, and I also played in a trio.

Though my mother continued to teach me Italian, piano and art over the years, I knew in my heart that I wasn't a master at any of them. I was still searching for something to excel in. What I enjoyed most was designing and building things. During those years my confidence in the work of my hands—conceiving, designing and constructing a creation—flourished. I excelled in math and architectural drafting. When reading magazines I'd pause to study building designs. Early evidence signaled that I was made to be an inventor or engineer. Because I loved to find out how things worked, I took a few physics classes at Pasadena City College that were not only good for my engineering mind but helped me master everyday challenges that presented some mechanical puzzle. *Why is the can opener stuck? What tool or process will remove this rusted lid? Why is this door not closing properly?*

That passion for mechanics would continue to grow in my heart.

SHAW PUMP

On summer vacations my dad employed me at his company, Shaw Pump, to earn a little extra money. Shaw Pump was located on Santa Fe Avenue in the dusty, smoky, industrial part of Los Angeles. The shop itself was dim and uninviting. I worked in the back, sweeping and putting away merchandise. Occasionally my father and I would have disagreements over how I was doing some part of my job. His disappointment in my performance chipped away at my self-confidence. Though I don't remember him ever speaking it aloud, I knew that my dad hoped I would enjoy the business so that he could pass it on to his only son. But I had no interest in pursuing it as a career.

Shaw Pump, manufacturing irrigation fittings and parts, was growing its portable aluminum irrigation business. We called the fittings StroLyte. My father dreamed that our success might extend to the eleven Western states. When my dad approached me about being a part of the growth, we decided that I would become a pilot to fly our salespeople around to distributors in these states. So, at nineteen, I enrolled in a class at the Rosemead Airport with an instructor named Sandy Banks. Sandy was an ex-aircraft carrier pilot who really knew his stuff. He took me up for my first flight in the Aeronca Champion, a small two-seater tail dragger.

I sat in the front seat like the command pilot and Sandy let me take the stick right away. We did a few landings and takeoffs so that I could get the feel of the machine. On my fifth, one-hour lesson, Sandy instructed me to pull over toward the hangar where several pilots were gathered.

He got out of the airplane and announced to all of those fellows, "Come and watch Bill on his first solo flight!"

They all cheered.

I was shocked. I asked, "You want me to fly the pattern by myself?"

Sandy confirmed, "Sure, you're ready. Go!"

Pushing the throttle forward, I taxied out to the runway. A long black strip stretched before me. Though I was safely on the ground, it occurred to me that I was in a machine that was about to lift me up in the air where my life would be in my own hands.

I wondered, *Do I really want to push the throttle forward?*

I glanced to see the crowd of guys standing at the hangar watching me. Waiting.

Could I turn back?

After several seconds, I pushed the throttle forward. Once I was airborne, I talked myself all the way around the pattern, remembering everything Sandy had taught me about altitude, position and speed.

As I made the last turn toward final approach I began to lose altitude a little faster. On the flights with Sandy, I'd always been afraid of coming in too low, causing Sandy to warn, "You're too high!" We'd fly the pattern again so I could take another shot at coming in low enough. This time I was on my own, and I was determined to come in low enough. The airplane settled nicely about a tenth of the way down the runway and I pulled the stick back enough to stall and settle the wheels.

"I made it! I made it!" I exclaimed loudly as I began to taxi down the runway to a stop.

Several moments after touchdown, though, I forgot to hold the stick back in the stall position and the airplane tail started to come up again. I quickly corrected this mistake. Thankfully, I don't think any of the pilots watching noticed. I pulled up to the hangar and all the guys clapped their hands and cheered. They broke out a bottle of beer and we all celebrated my achievement.

CHAPTER 2
Companions for Life

I was attending Pasadena City College when I met Lorraine. We had both taken a class called "Marriage." At the time I was hanging around with a fellow musician named Dick Blum, and we'd signed up for the marriage class as a lark.

One morning I walked into the room and dipped down the aisle of seats to reach my assigned seat. Three rows down I passed a dark-haired, pretty young lady. Our eyes met but I didn't say anything.

After class that day I asked Dick if he knew who she was.

He said, "Yeah, she hangs around with the group of girls in a campus sorority. Her name is Lorraine Vasi."

I thought she must be Italian. From my early lessons with my mother, I remembered how to say, "Buongiorno," for good morning. The next day, as I passed her on my way to my seat, I gathered my courage to say it as I passed by. She just looked up at me and gave me a weak smile.

The next day I said "Buongiorno" again.

This time she responded with "Good morning."

Unfortunately, as I asked around, I found out she had a boyfriend named Paul. So I became discouraged.

Soon after, I was giving a party for some of my friends at my home in San Marino. Dick Blum and I invited a lot of friends from school. He invited Lorraine and Paul. I remember greeting them with two other couples as they arrived at the door that Saturday night.

I said to Lorraine and she walked in, "I know you from school."

She responded with a smile. We chatted a bit and I could tell she was going to be friendly.

Back at school we continued to have casual conversations, and I learned that she liked the musician Stan Kenton, as I did. This impressed me because it took an unusual ear to enjoy his modern sounds. His band was composed of outstanding musicians, and it took great skill and talent to play those complex compositions.

A few months later, Dick and Lorraine and I were on a triple-date to go dancing at the Palladium in Hollywood. The next week, Lorraine told me how she watched me on the dance floor with my date and wished that she could have been dancing with me. I hoped that meant what I thought it meant. That same evening, when we were both on dates with other people, we shared more casual conversation that helped us become acquainted with each other.

During summer break I mustered the courage to give Lorraine a call and invited her to go with me to a small club on Normandy Avenue in Hollywood. Stan Kenton and the band would be playing there for one night. She said yes. The club was small, the room was crowded and the Cokes we were drinking were expensive. I didn't care because I finally had a date with Lorraine where she was my date! We had a great time that night. Because we'd already been developing a friendship, I felt free to give her a quick kiss good night as I walked her to her door that evening. Several dates followed and it wasn't long before I knew I was in love with her. It took me several months, but after returning from a date, parked in front of her house in my 1935 Ford, I told her I loved her. She let me know she was falling in love with me also.

In those last minutes and hours of our dates, parked in front of her home, we began discussing what it would might be like to be married. When it got late, Lorraine's father, Frank Vasi, would turn on the porch light to let us know it was time for her to come in the house.

We'd known each other for about four months when I invited Lorraine to come with our family to our mountain cabin at Big Bear Lake. She was given a little space curtained off in the adjoining room next to the kitchen. My parents slept in the cabin's one bedroom, and I had the outside back porch all to myself. I learned later that she was impressed with my attentive conversations with my mother that she heard through the thin walls as I helped my mother prepare breakfast in the kitchen.

One evening during our Big Bear weekend, I took Lorraine for a ride around the lake in the family car. We stopped at a couple of romantic places to look out over the peaceful lake at night. When we returned to the cabin, before going inside, I popped the question.

"Will you marry me?" I queried.

"Yes," she confirmed, her eyes sparkling.

Though I knew what her answer would be, I was relieved and delighted to hear it.

I didn't tell my parents of our decision that night. We decided Lorraine was going to tell her parents when she got home and I would check in with her to hear how they received the announcement. She said they were pleased and didn't make very much of it. So, the following night, I told my parents.

My mother was delighted, but my father was reluctant to give his approval. He kept saying over and over, "You're too young." He also pointed out that we'd met just ten months earlier.

He demanded, "How are you going to support her on a Shaw Pump shipping clerk's salary?"

Lorraine and I were both disappointed.

My father, twelve years older than my mother, had gotten married when he was thirty-eight. I insisted to him that both Lorraine and I were ready for marriage. I would turn twenty-one in the spring, and we would be married in May. Though Lorraine was only eighteen, she was eager and willing to launch into her future with me.

Thankfully, my father came around a few weeks later and even became very supportive.

When the Korean War erupted, I was in the Air Force Weather Reserve. So it looked doubtful that I would be able to stay out of the service. That prospect did little to deter Lorraine and me from continuing our planning for our marriage. Our wedding wasn't too expensive, but it was memorable. The ceremony was at Saint Matthew's Catholic Church of Pasadena, and the reception was held at The Athletic Club. After punch and cake, we were off on our honeymoon to the Grand Canyon.

Lorraine and I had a wonderful time during our three-day stay at this magnificent natural wonder of the world. On the way home I wanted her to see the desert shack in which I'd spent so many memorable days with my father and uncles in the Turtle Mountains of California.

The journey was an all-day trip from the Grand Canyon. As we approached the shack, we traveled sixteen miles of dirt roads before turning off the pavement into the middle of nowhere. We arrived just before dark.

On our trip I'd shared with Lorraine my dream of raising blackberries in the flat open valley land nearby. At that time this land was available for $3 per acre from the government on what was called "school land." Unfortunately, it was not a very inviting prospect to Lorraine.

The cabin was intact, with the bedrolls neatly hanging from the ceiling to keep the animals from destroying them. I got them down, and we made up our beds. The wood-burning stove provided the heat to warm up the food we'd brought. By the time it got dark, mice and rats were scurrying around the room. We decided not to spend the night in the shack and slept instead in my 1947 Chevy. The next day I took my unhappy bride directly home to our new house at 829 Broadway in San Gabriel.

During our engagement I'd searched and found a small home that we could afford with the down payment I'd saved up. The two-bedroom home, situated on a large lot, cost $8,750—20 percent down and payments of $50 per month. Over the next two years I expanded the home's bathroom and small bedroom. I also built a two-car garage with the structural capacity to build an apartment over it one day.

OUR CALLING

We started our family early. Eleven months after our 1952 wedding day, Eugene (Gene) Frank Ashe was born. Our second son, Donald Leon Ashe, was born almost two and a half years later. After Eugene was born, we decided we needed to agree about God and what we would teach our children. Since I was a Protestant by default, as a result of my family's history, and she was a Catholic for the same reasons, we decided it would be important for us to find common spiritual ground so we could share a faith we could pass on to our children.

We began by looking to our respective churches for advice. Lorraine arranged a meeting at the Catholic church where we were invited to attend a class with other young married couples. My only real recollection is that this meeting was dry and solemn. In the meantime, I was convinced we should start to study the Bible since most people of faith said that this is where they found truth. We were both seekers, so God's promise came true. Searching the Scriptures, we read, "Seek the LORD while he may be found, call upon him while he is near" (Isaiah 55:6). We also studied Hebrews 11:6: "And without faith it is impossible to please him. For whoever would draw near to God must believe that he exists and that he rewards those who seek him."

Most of the preachers we'd heard used the Bible as the premise of their preaching. We decided to attend the local Catholic church and find out what type of Bible studies were being offered. To our surprise the local priest told us there were none. They were only teaching catechism classes. We attended one or two, but they disappointed us. So we pressed on and learned more about the Bible on our own.

At age twenty-two I had a life-changing experience. I had joined the Optimist Club of South San Gabriel as an employee of Shaw Pump and Supply. One of the owners of L & J Truck Lines, John Craig, was my sponsor. He picked up pumps and products for shipments at Shaw Pump where I worked as the shipping clerk. He was a gregarious, outgoing guy, always having fun. During my second year as a member I was elected president of the Optimist Club. When the nomination and election took place, I didn't know if I could stand up in front of the whole group and lead the meeting as others did. But the Lord pushed me a little, and I mustered the courage to accept the job. I quickly overcame my stage fright and enjoyed the leadership experience. I discovered I could hold the group's attention and even make them laugh.

I had been married to Lorraine for two years, and she noticed the change as my confidence flourished and my social networks expanded. She fit right in at the social functions. The optimist philosophy fit me well. I had always been one to find the best in each situation. To me, a half-empty glass was always half full.

All of these experiences were shaping my personality for what God had prepared for me. My growing social confidence would help me serve in the family of God by encouraging people to have compassion on the poor. I was also beginning to discover ways to utilize my skills with water pumps to make a positive difference in the lives of those who were poor.

About this time, as we were seeking the Lord, I was watching television one evening when Lorraine was out and caught a preacher talking about the prophecy of "the Day of the Lord." He had my undivided attention. The children were sleeping and there were no distractions.

At the conclusion of this warning prophecy, he announced, "The Second Coming of the Lord is only five or ten or fifteen years away, so you better get your house in order."

Looking up from his live audience, peering into the camera to address television viewers, he commanded, "If you have never asked the Lord to forgive you of your sins, it is time to put a peg down and pray right now for the Lord to forgive you of you sins."

That's exactly what I did. Though there was no bolt of lightning or angel visitation, I felt a sense of peace that what I'd done was good for my soul.

At the time I figured Lorraine had done this in her past, maybe years ago during a catechism class, so I didn't think it was important to explain what I had done. Honestly, I didn't want her to know I was just catching on to the fact that Jesus could forgive my sins personally. My concept had always been that Jesus was the Savior of everybody, automatically.

I began sharing with her how the Lord led me to a Christian businessman, Bob Hayward, who needed pumps we were selling at Shaw Pump. His business was only two blocks away from ours. It wasn't long after my first or second sales visit that he brought up a subject he'd recently been considering, "Who am I? Where my going? Why am I here?" These were the kinds of questions I'd begun to ask in high school, and they were still stirring in my soul as well. So we had some interesting conversations about "religion" over brown bag lunches in his office. It was a nice diversion from the pump problem discussions!

He finally invited me to attend an evening discussion at his house. He said a "guy" from his church was leading this event. This guy turned out to be the preacher Dr. Robert Schaper. I found out later that Bob had alerted him that I was coming, that we'd discussed eternal things, but that he didn't think I was a Christian. At the conclusion of the meeting, Dr. Schaper was explaining how important it was to ask Jesus, in a prayer of confession, to come into your life, forgive you of your sins, and be the Lord of your life. I just nodded in agreement.

I began attending services at Bethany Church where Dr. Schaper preached. Lorraine was attending a Catholic church, and we'd share what we were each learning over lunch on Sundays.

Because I wanted to clear the air with Dr. Schaper and be sure about what I believed, I asked to meet with him to share what was on my heart. One weekday, just before lunch, I met with him in the quiet fellowship hall at the church. Not long after we sat down, he asked me if I had ever asked Jesus into my life. I assured him that I had, recounting what I'd done in response to the invitation from the television preacher. He was glad that I was born again but wanted me to tell the whole church of my experience to validate my faith. He pointed out how Jesus asked His followers to make it public. So the following Sunday he invited me to share from the platform. He called me forward and I gave my simple story. After the service people in the church were very open and friendly, ready to accept me into the family of God. This was such a wonderful experience that I shared it with Lorraine that afternoon.

She was still somewhat skeptical but agreed to come to church with me to see what it was all about. As we began to attend together, the gospel became clearer to her. One Sunday morning in church as Dr. Schaper concluded his sermon, he asked if anyone would like to come forward and receive Christ as Savior and Lord. The Holy Spirit led Lorraine to do just that. I immediately followed her, and we both shed tears of joy at what God was doing in our lives.

The people were friendly and gave us big hugs as they welcomed us into the fellowship at Bethany Church. Dr. Schaper made sure that we got into the Bible as soon as possible. We look back now and appreciate his wisdom to help us become growing new Christians. It protected us from the call of sin and the pursuits of this world's things to lead us away from the kingdom of God (Romans 12:2).

And he put me in charge of a fourth-grade boys' Sunday school class and Lorraine became active in an adult Sunday school class.

In a sermon on prayer, Dr. Schaper said, "If you're not praying now, a good place to start is at every meal." This impressed both Lorraine and me, and we have followed his advice ever since. Our children learned to pray as we prayed at meals. We were also learning to have Bible studies in our home with the children. They were not always consistent, but it was definitely a good time of training.

In the young adults' Sunday school class Lorraine was a sponge, soaking up all she could about how to "set your mind on the things of the Spirit" and avoid the things in the flesh. The Sunday school classes met before the church service, and we enjoyed wonderful sermons by Dr. Schaper every Sunday.

Our two boys adapted to this new routine. Eugene was a participant in the four-year-old Sunday school class and Don spent time in the nursery. We soon became so enthused about our new Christian life that we began attending the Sunday evening service. Sometimes we would also go to the Wednesday prayer meeting. The prayer meeting was a good place to learn how the church prays for the missionaries on the field and for the needy. Bethany Church was a strong missionary-sending church. We sent 50 percent of our church budget to the mission field.

The Holy Spirit was impressing on our hearts the importance of the Great Commission: "Go and make disciples of all nations, baptizing them in the name of the Father and of the son and of the Holy Spirit" (Matthew 28:19).

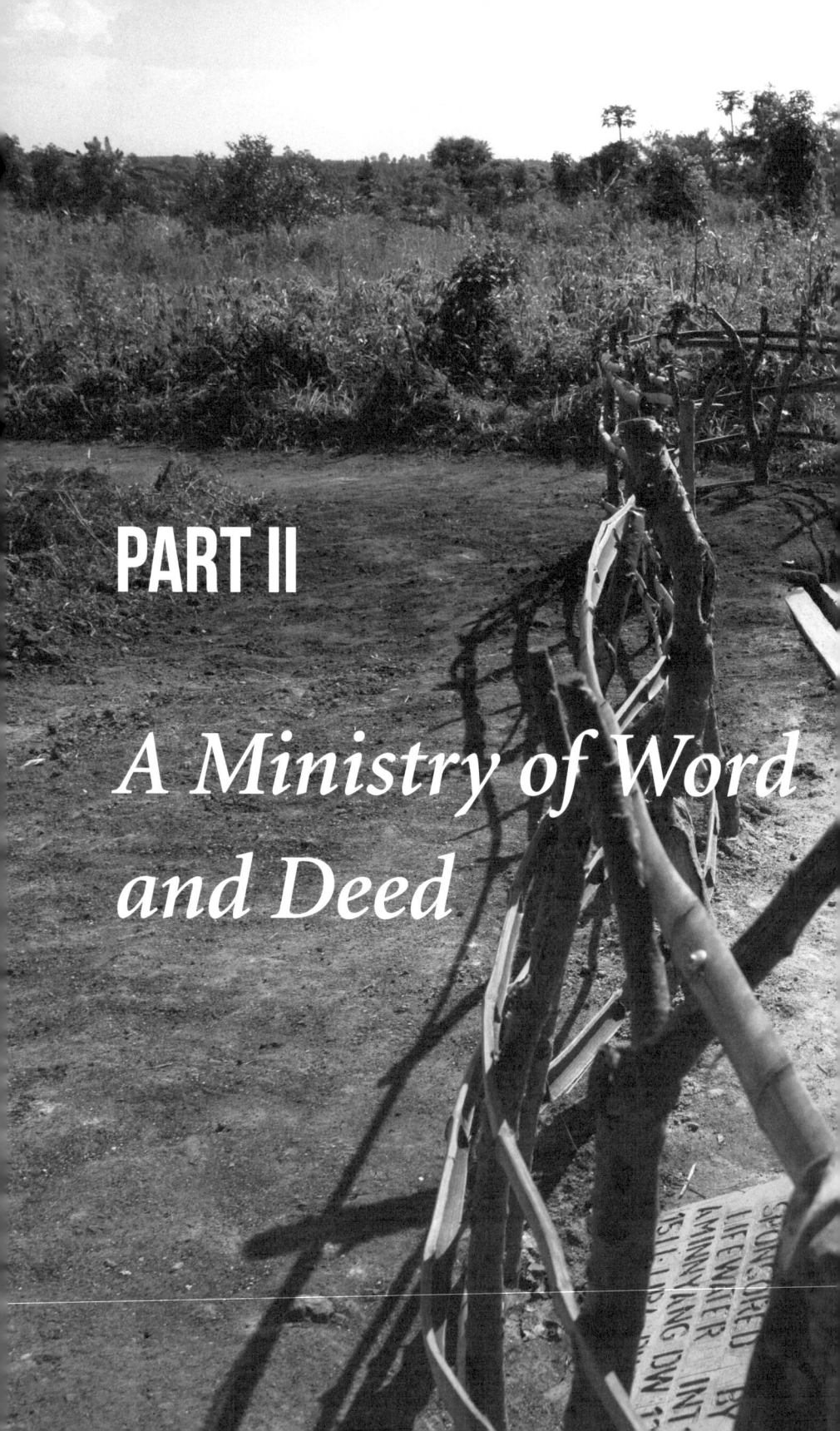

PART II

A Ministry of Word and Deed

CHAPTER 3
Seeds of a Ministry

Our family was growing, and our interest in missions was expanding. I was fortunate to have Lorraine, who was doing an excellent job as a young mother raising our children during the daytime while I was at work. As it was with many young couples, she had the whole day with them while I was only home in the evenings. In addition, as I became involved in the church's ministry, she was covering for my family absence during times when I was involved with kingdom service. The Lord helped us keep a good balance between my time away and home time with the family.

In 1957 we decided to sell our home and buy one closer to our church where two other families from Bethany Church lived. They were the families of Bob Hayward and Jim Petersen, men who'd become close friends of mine. Although they had become Christians a year or two before me, we were all learning what it meant to be active "word and deed" believers (1 John 3:18; Colossians 3:17). According to John, "word and deed" believers put God's truth into action.

The new house was situated in a wonderful neighborhood in Pasadena just next to the west border of Sierra Madre. It was called Upper Hastings Ranch. There were about two hundred tract homes constructed after the Second World War. Many had GI loans at an interest rate of 4 percent, a desirable loan rate at the time. We fell in love with it. It was less than two miles to our beloved Bethany and new circle of Christian friends.

The house was listed as being "for sale by owner." Unfortunately, we made the classic mistake of falling in love with a home we desperately wanted to buy before we had sold our existing home. My parents helped us by putting up the money for about two months. Eventually we had to sell below our asking price since we had moved into the new home and left the old one vacant. It was a buyers' market. Nonetheless, we felt the Lord wanted us to have this home.

Jim Peterson and I decided we would do door-to-door evangelism in our neighborhood. There were two hundred homes as our field to make disciples. We devised a simple survey as our "cold turkey" introduction to this neighborhood evangelism experience.

The survey had three questions:

1. Do you believe in God?
2. Do you believe the Bible is the Word of God?
3. Do you understand the gospel?

Every Saturday morning we would begin our adventure. We dressed in sport clothes without ties. We would knock on the door and announce, "We are your neighbors from Rexford and are taking a small survey in Upper Hastings Ranch. Would you be willing to answer three questions this morning?"

The reactions we received varied from a quick, definitive "No" to "What church are you from?" to "Are you Jehovah Witnesses?" We persevered door after door until we heard "Yes, I'll answer your survey." When we received a "Yes," we would quickly go through our questions. If they understood the gospel, we would say thank you and move on.

But every Saturday someone would say, "Understand the gospel? Not really."

This opened the door for us to share four simple Bible verses.

We'd query, "Would you let us show you?"

When we were invited into the home, it was often by a young couple confused about life and eager to hear if there was an answer to "Who am I?" "Where am I going?" and "Why am I here?" One couple, in particular, was moved to tears as they joined us in a sinner's prayer of repentance and an invitation for the Lord Jesus Christ to come into their lives as their Lord and Savior.

RECEIVING THE GIFT OF ANNA

One Saturday, during our evangelism campaign in the neighborhood, we came upon a couple who were adopting two children from Greece. The McKees explained how this was going to happen with a lady from Pasadena, Mrs. Pampeyan, whose close Christian friend was running an orphanage in Katirini, Northern Greece. There were still four children eligible to be adopted into Christian homes in America. They explained to us that these kids were unspoken for. There were three young boys, and the fourth was a twelve-year-old girl who was probably going to be left behind because of her age. This girl was named Soultana Lazaridou. Lorraine and I prayed about this situation. Though we really wanted a baby, the Holy Spirit was drawing us to consider Soultana.

We were moved by her situation and began wondering if the Lord was inviting us to bring this girl into our family. As Lorraine and I prayed more about the situation, we became convinced the Holy Spirit was telling us this was the right thing to do. So we started the process to adopt her.

I began by visiting with Mrs. Pampeyan. She explained to me that Anna, as she was called, came from a very poor family. Her father had been a farmer and an evangelical preacher, but had died when she was two years old. Her mother lived in a very small mud-brick home in disrepair. Her health was so poor that she could not take proper care of her two youngest daughters. At the conclusion of our discussion, I asked if I could pray about our decision in this matter. She agreed. Though she didn't tell me until later, she watched me out of the corner of her eye and listened to me as I prayed. This gave her a peace in her heart that I would make a good father for Anna. The orphanage in Katirini sent Lorraine and me a two- by three-inch, black-and-white picture of Anna, which was our first visual connection to her.

Because there were complications between Greek laws and California laws, the adoption process took a full year.

In June 1959, after a thirty-six-hour trip with two stops, she arrived at the Los Angeles International Airport. Together with the Pampeyans, we were there for the first time. She was also escorting the three younger boys who were being adopted by others. One was still in diapers. She had been responsible for the two-day journey halfway around the world. The experience had obviously been difficult for her, but she tried to stay cheerful, as was her nature. She spoke no English, and I had only learned a few Greek words. But smiles and hugs communicated the joy we all had as she began her first day with the Ashe family.

WATCHING ANNA FLOURISH

When she was twenty, Anna married a Greek man, George Kefalas, and the two became actively engaged in Bible studies and outreach projects. Sometime later, a congregation of the Greek Evangelical Church had its start in their home. Today it is active and contributing to the proclamation of the gospel in both Greek and English. George was an assistant pastor, and their sons, Michael and William, were eventually also active in leadership roles in the church.

Anna and George chose to go back to Greece and visit the orphanage she called home for three of her preadolescent years. Lorraine and I joined them on this first visit back to her roots in 1990. When we arrived at the "orphanage," the new owners of the home, people she'd never met, greeted us. It was no longer being operated as a children's home. They did allow us to come in so she could show us the room where she slept.

As she walked into the room and pointed toward the place where her bed had been, she exclaimed, "Everything looks so much smaller!"

This experience challenged Anna and George to join with others assisting orphans in Greece and the surrounding areas. They also helped organize some of the orphans who had been adopted into American families, and this group became The Benjamin Child Support Society. The central focus was to find children in poverty and sponsor them by identifying compassionate donors in America who would support homes in Greece that would give them a stable foundation and love. The ministry grew in remarkable ways.

GROWING IN FAITH

I always knew my father to be an honest man. He was a fierce competitor in business but always ethical. Occasionally he played golf, but otherwise had no hobbies. He attended church to please my mother. She read the Bible to me on occasion, but wasn't well informed about what to read or how to study.

After Lorraine and I had been Christians for a few years, I had the opportunity to share the gospel with my father. We were sitting together on the living room couch in our home in Upper Hastings Ranch without others present. I told him I'd heard many stories from his brothers that led me to believe his parents were true believers. I asked him point-blank, "Have you ever asked Jesus to forgive you of your sins and asked him to be your Lord and Savior?"

He answered, "Yes, when I was a boy."

That knowledge comforted me when my father died in 1977.

My sister Janet lived with my mother in her home in Arcadia for a few years prior to her death. Janet would bring Mom to church every Sunday at Christ Community Church, where our son Donald was the pastor. Janet and mother both made a profession of faith there. She always took special delight in her grandson, who has a special gift for preaching the Word. After their profession of faith, my mom and Janet were baptized on a Sunday afternoon that has become a treasured memory for our family. Though her husband preceded her in death by almost two decades, my mother lived to just two months short of her ninety-first birthday.
I am confident in the grace and mercy of God our Father for my father's salvation. I know he and my mother practiced a very moral lifestyle. They conditioned us to believe in God and live by biblical principles. I'm sure their influence affected my desire to learn more about who Jesus was and is. I am thankful to God that I have trusted in the message, which still applies today. And I'm encouraged by Peter's words: "He will bring you a message through which you and all your household will be saved" (Acts 11:14).

I am so very thankful my entire household has been saved.

OUR FIRST PROJECT

In 1962, during a Sunday school class, Ken Stroman—the USA director of Mexican Fellowship Orphanage—introduced Lorraine and me to the orphanage in Ensenada, Mexico. I'd been a Christian for six years and had been gripped by the "therefore" lifestyle guidelines in Romans 12. Paul appeals to believers to worship God, not just with their minds and hearts, but with their whole bodies. "I appeal to you therefore, brothers and sisters, by the mercies of God, to present your bodies as a living sacrifice, holy and acceptable to God, which is your spiritual worship" (Romans 12:1, NRSV).

Lorraine and I heard Ken was inviting us to worship God more deeply by responding to the needs of the poor.

That moment, when our hearts were gripped by the mission and vision of the orphanage, would be a memory to which I'd return during difficult times in the years to come.

Ken explained to our class that, even though a well had recently been built in the community, they were still carrying their water long distances in buckets while the well was waiting for a new pump. He'd been advised that a windmill could be installed that would pump the water directly up into a tank to be installed a little above the orphanage on the hillside. This would allow the water supply to flow under enough pressure to give tap water to all three buildings.

He expressed this need to all of us in the Sunday school class. Of course my ears rang as I sensed the Holy Spirit speaking to me. This was a special opportunity, since our family company, Shaw Pump, sells windmills. After the class I introduced myself. He was delighted and explained that he'd priced some windmills in Mexico that had been very expensive.

"How much do they cost?" he asked, hesitantly.

"Let's not worry about the cost," I counseled. "I think we could raise the funds through this Sunday school class."

His eyes lit up.

"That would be wonderful," he gushed.

Thinking about the work of installation, I queried, "Do you have people who could help us install it?"

"Oh yes," he promised, "plenty of helpers!"

Ken was thrilled that the Holy Spirit had orchestrated this creative solution to the important need facing the orphanage.

The next Sunday I made the announcement to our Sunday school class that the purchase of this windmill would be an opportunity for us to help these orphan children in San Carlos Canyon, Baja Mexico. If our class would buy it, I offered, I would personally supervise the installation. Thankfully, their response was enthusiastic!

As the weeks passed, the donations were slowly rolling in. But the Lord was speaking to my heart, urging, "You supply the rest." So Lorraine and I made up the balance of the funds. The day after I called to let him know we had a windmill for him, he called to say that they were ready to receive and install the windmill as soon as possible.

Early one Friday morning, Ken and Maria, the woman who ran the orphanage, arrived at Shaw Pumps' back door in a red pickup truck to fetch their prize. We loaded all the windmill parts and tools into the truck and set out for the Mexican border, praying that the border guards would let us through without a bribe request.

Unfortunately, we were stopped by the Mexican border guards at the crossing south of San Diego. They asked us about the brand-new stuff in our pickup truck. Maria explained that it was for an orphanage and begged them to let us pass without any "import taxes." The guard, reluctant, insisted that we needed to pay. As she pled with the guard, Ken and I prayed silently. After several minutes, the captain at the station appeared in the doorway and ordered, "Let them go!" Since the conversation was in Spanish, I didn't find out what was said until we drove away. As they faded into the distance of the truck's rearview mirror, Maria explained how the captain exercised his authority over the young border guard by telling him to let us go. This was another validation to us that the Lord was in charge and clearing the way for us with special demonstrations of His power.

As we drove away we sang and praised the Lord all the way through Tijuana. We'd expected that this "import tax" could be a sizable expense, quite possibly one beyond our pocketbooks. If it had been necessary for us to fill out the papers and pay the import duty at the border station, we would have had to stay overnight in San Diego before passing. Thankfully we were able to carry on and arrived at the orphanage in the afternoon, giving us plenty of time to unload the windmill components at the well site in preparation for the installation the next day.

We all slept in one large room, throwing sleeping bags and straw mats on the cement floor, like all the children. At thirty-one years old, my body could still take the hard floor! However, I still didn't sleep well, anticipating some sort of problem installing that windmill. There were hundreds of pieces to put together, and I was hoping they were all there and easy to identify. After a breakfast of beans, rice and tortillas, we set out for the windmill site.

Instruction schematic in hand, I dumped the bag of parts on the ground, letting the children identify and gather all the similar pieces. I had many willing hands, and the kids delighted in the opportunity to help with the enterprise. Several young men, whom Ken had contacted weeks before, were also ready to help with the heavy work.

It took us several hours to piece the windmill together in a horizontal position, assembling it entirely on the ground. When it was time to erect it vertically over the well, we rigged a long rope and a pole with a pulley and used a pickup truck for power. I supervised the erection of this windmill as several Mexican men guided the lift. Keeping the rope tight, as the truck pulled, prevented the windmill from moving past vertical and tumbling over. When it slowly rose to a vertical position, everybody cheered. I quickly installed the anchor bolts in the steel tower legs that were already installed in the ground. This ensured that the wind, or an accident, wouldn't cause it to fall over.

There was just one thing wrong. As I peeked into the rearview mirror, the name "Dempster" was inverted. The tail of the windmill had been assembled upside down!

When we all noticed that the tail had been installed upside down, laughter erupted from everyone but me. This was a big embarrassment. I'd been billed as the expert coming from the United States to install this windmill. I needed a plan.

It was late afternoon and the sky would be completely dark within a few hours. To take the windmill back down, just to reassemble the tail, would be dangerous and time-consuming. We had several hours of work left to complete the installation, pouring cement into the foundation legs as well as connecting the pump and pipes. I decided that the best option was to leave it as it was and finish the installation. The tail would work just as well with the printing upside down.

The Lord used that mishap to teach me a very important spiritual lesson. When we'd begun the project that day, I'd not paused to invite the group to pray. All through the operation I'd been accepting the praise of men who viewed me as the big expert. The Lord was not receiving the glory for what He had done. This experience has served me well since that day when the Lord taught me to exercise humility in kingdom service. Whenever I would think of it, the Lord would bring to mind Zechariah 4:6, "This is the word of the LORD to Zerubbabel: 'Not by might nor by power, but by my Spirit,' says the LORD Almighty." Through that humbling experience God taught me what Paul also learned, "My grace is sufficient for you, for my power is made perfect in weakness" (2 Corinthians 12:9). Since then I've discovered many times over that God's will is accomplished because He chooses to work in willing, but weak, people.

Several years later I was flying to another assignment in Baja and we passed directly over San Carlos Canyon, where that first windmill still stood. The pilot buzzed the area so we could get a glimpse. Though I was the only one aware of it from the plane, I peered out the window to see the windmill with the upside-down tail. It stood as a monument to my error and a constant reminder of the true source of my spiritual strength.

I made several trips back to the orphanage after being exposed to the great need there. Lorraine accompanied me on a few occasions. Each time Ken would show us new opportunities to help the children with their spiritual and physical needs. It's what had launched my passion for "word and deed" projects.

Throughout the years the Holy Spirit has reminded me that when I give the glory to the Lord, I obtain a private spiritual blessing between Him and me. Praise His name!

In 1963, when Gene was ten, Don was eight, and Anna was eighteen, we welcomed Kevin, our fourth and final child, into our family.

THE MINISTRY DEVELOPS, 1966–1977

For thirteen years our family had been firmly committed to helping people who were poor through our family pump company and water management skills. In 1977, though, I began to wake up to what the Lord might make of our family ministry. I knew that half the world was without safe water to drink and thirty thousand people died daily from drinking contaminated water. I was convinced that we could do more in this world of hurt!

Colossians 4:5 exhorts believers to "make the most of every opportunity." But for thirteen years I'd not determined to make more of our water ministry to the poor. The Lord began to make it clear to me that He'd developed special skills in my life that I should employ where He directed. I began to call the moments when these opportunities became clear "It Just So Happened" events!

For years I'd been working for my father at Shaw Pump and Supply on a shipping clerk's salary, while slowly working my way up to purchasing Agent. Lorraine and I were trying to raise our family and had few free weekends to go to Mexico. Yet we knew there were opportunities to help the orphanages, Christian camps, missionary homes and schools that I'd been advising. Though I squeezed in trips when I could, I'd not been able to give them the personal attention they needed. I wanted to do more.

When the word got out in the Christian missionary community that Bill Ashe was willing to help with anything related to pumps and water supplies, people and organizations with needs would track me down at Shaw Pump. It was the Holy Spirit's way of giving me opportunities to assist poor people for kingdom purposes. Every now and then the Lord would open the door for me to spend a weekend visiting a site and correcting some problem that others couldn't solve when the remedy available through local commercial companies seemed too expensive.

In several instances, mission compound water systems that had been modified over time had become a terrible tangle of inadequate pipes. They'd been constructed by well-meaning handymen from mission groups who knew just enough about gluing plastic pipes together to be dangerous. Most of the time missionaries complained, "There's not enough pressure!" The pipes were often too small, creating friction losses that kept the volume from being sufficient. It often took a new pump, or a pressure tank, and larger piping to correct the problem. In these cases, I would often leave my drawings and shopping lists for others to implement the changes I suggested. Thankfully only a few projects required a second trip to find out what had gone wrong with their original systems.

The missionaries at Luminaria Christian School were having pump problems that no one was able to diagnose. Using my eyes, ears and experience, I was able to recognize the problem. The pump's labored growl, while trying to move more water than it was built for, told me the builders had used the wrong pipe size.

At Rancho Sordomudo, an orphanage for deaf children, a freshly drilled well needed a new pump. Local Mexican suppliers wanted to charge these missionaries about twice what it should have cost. I helped them through the problem and got the pump installed. They were able to apply this wonderful savings to other much-needed supplies for the orphanage. Over the years Ed and Margaret Everett, the directors of the orphanage, became good friends of mine as we partnered to keep the pumps, tanks and pipes at their facility working. This relationship was yet another confirmation from the Lord that I should be using the skills and experience I'd been given for kingdom purposes.

A rapidly growing church facility at Sierra Azul in Tecati, Mexico, needed a well drilled and a pump installed. This church longed to supply the entire community in the area with access to safe water. Randy Fain, a Christian friend I met through Shaw Pump, was in the pump business in Escondido. After some careful planning and difficult border crossings with the equipment, he drilled a well and installed the pump in the community. The community rejoiced over the new supply of safe water. The Lord's presence was evident as communist threats, other political opposition and drilling hazards were avoided.

Graciously, the Lord continued to show me the great need and offer opportunities to help the poor. I also felt the Holy Spirit nudging me to enlist other Christians to help. It became apparent that the opportunities to help the poorest of the poor by meeting this basic human need were limitless.

CHAPTER 4
The Birth of Lifewater

In 1977, 2.5 billion people, half of the world, were trying survive with unsafe water. The need represented, to me, an unlimited opportunity for Christians to serve the poor. That year, God awoke me to "make the most of the time" by finding others with a desire to bring safe drinking water to the rural poor. So, as a family, we formed a new organization called Lifewater.

I informed some of my business friends and people in other ministries of our desire to begin a Christian training ministry that would help the rural poor develop safe drinking water supplies. We'd use professional water resource management specialists to design cost-effective remedies. I read many mission magazines to learn as much as I could about how ministries were resolving these problems. I contacted staff at World Vision, Food for the Hungry, World Concern, Compassion International and a few others to learn how they operated. Each of these ministries was addressing water project requests from staff in the field with in-house water experts or outsourced contractors.

Since water is the most basic human need, and is so intimately connected to public health, I expected to discover good strategies and designs in ministries serving the poor overseas. To my dismay I was discovering many failed projects. These findings led me to believe that the highest and best calling for Lifewater would be to offer these organizations the professional assistance of a team of Lifewater volunteers who were experts. I expected that these professionals would be able to analyze ministries' requests and offer designs and procedures to meet needs in the most cost-effective manner. The overall objective was always to be able to train missionaries in the field in how to continue safe water practices.

With this new concept in mind, I asked these organizations if they could utilize our services at Lifewater to help them design and implement water development projects. Again to my disappointment, I had less than enthusiastic responses from these agencies. I sensed they perceived Lifewater to be a confusing fit for their image and identity in the field.

I had discovered an unspoken fear among agencies about whose water project experts would be perceived in the villages as those who were doing the work. These agencies were establishing a presence in these villages and didn't want the local people confused about who was serving them. At first I thought this was petty. But after thinking it through, I realized it might be the best approach after all. Cross-cultural relationships are difficult at best. The people need to relate to and negotiate with one outside organization.

Because this concern was inhibiting Lifewater building relationships with organizations as a subcontractor, I suggested that Lifewater volunteers doing a job for any agency would wear their hats and T-shirts so that Lifewater would remain anonymous.

A DOOR OPENS IN HAITI, 1980

One Sunday, Mr. Dave Graffenberger came to our Sunday school class at Bethany Church. Dave represented Men for Missions International, the laymen's branch of One Mission Society International (OMS). This men's ministry gathered men from all over the United States and sent them to Haiti, where they supported OMS work projects. When Dave addressed our class, he described the great need for safe drinking water in rural areas of Cap-Haïtien. Tragically, it was commonplace for these communities to drink from open surface water sources. As a result, waterborne diseases ran rampant through the population. Dave asked us to pray that God would send someone to develop a strategy for correcting this situation.

If ever the Holy Spirit was touching my heart, this was the day and this was the moment! Lorraine was sitting beside me. A single glance between us confirmed that this was something we could do. Several weeks later we flew to Houston to join a group of eight more couples traveling together to Haiti. After landing in Port-au-Prince, we took a bumpy all-day bus ride to Cap-Haïtien. Our bus driver was Harold Brown, who was also the OMS mission director in Haiti. He stopped along the way to show us interesting sites and places where water well repairs were needed. Over the next few days, at the OMS compound in Cap-Haïtien, we worked together to plan our various tasks. My assignment was to meet with Les Babcock, the OMS compound engineer. He kept the diesel generators running and the water flowing from the compound's pump to the fifteen buildings on its five-acre site.

Lorraine and I, along with the other couples, were privileged to spend a wonderful week learning about the OMS mission strategy. We visited field sites and observed the fruit of their ministry. Some of our group served as teachers that week and some helped with construction. All who felt called were able to help in some capacity. One day we visited a church in the Plaine Du Nord where the practice of voodoo was rampant. Sadly prevalent throughout most of Haiti, this particular area was a focal point for witch doctors and others engaged in occult practices.

We arrived at the church as night fell. Driving through the community in the big blue bus, we were startled to see young men with faces painted white—white to symbolize a zombie! They were waving toy guns at us and banging on the sides of the bus. Suddenly, spiritual warfare took on new meaning for me. I found myself praying for our safety, but even more so for the lives of these troubled young men. With a silent prayer of thanksgiving, we arrived at the church as a worship service was already in progress.

The church was a one-room, cement-block building thirty feet wide and fifty feet long. Dangling from the middle of its tin roof was one light bulb, providing the only light for the two guitarists leading worship from the front. A small generator running out back ran both the single lightbulb and the amp from which their music blasted. Right in the middle of worship, the generator stopped, leaving us in silent, total blackness. Of course the Haitians knew just what to do, and within minutes the power was restored.

Lorraine and I were deeply moved as we witnessed these people, who owned so little of this world's goods, celebrating God's grace and love with joy and enthusiasm. She and I were chosen to give a testimony at the close of the service. What a joy to express our love for the Lord! Clearly, these beautiful lives were the finest fruits of OMS Ministries. In the midst of a desperately poor village, pressed in on every side by satanic darkness, these Christian men and women shone as lights in the darkness.

During our time in Cap-Haïtien, we were also privileged to go out into the more rural communities with OMS leadership. We gathered in teams of three, one couple and one OMS missionary to translate, to pass out tracts door-to-door. While Lorraine and I were passing out tracts and invitations to the Sunday service, a petite elderly widow, whose deep wrinkles bore the testimony of many hard years, invited us into her home. She lived there with a very young girl in her care, and we guessed this was her granddaughter. Her home was a flimsy, ten-foot-square shack, consisting of branches, slats and cardboard strapped and tacked together, with only palm tree fronds for a roof. This humble home was furnished with a small table and a chair that stood in the center of the dirt floor. She apologized to us for not having some gift to offer. She explained that she was very grateful for our efforts to help her community. She said that all she had to give was a song. With that, she began to sing one of the Christian hymns she had learned, with genuine devotion ringing through each note. Lorraine and I were so overwhelmed and moved that we had a hard time standing in the presence of this holy event! As this tiny lady sang from her soul, it was entirely evident that the Holy Spirit was gifting Lorraine and me with an incredible experience. This woman clearly had "living water" welling up within her, and it spilled freely out onto us.

Les Babcock, the compound engineer, and I became friends over the next few days. He helped me to grasp the big picture regarding water problems throughout Haiti, particularly the problems for rural villagers forced to drink contaminated water. Contamination was often caused by wells being left as open pits. In addition, wells were often very far apart, and there was no sense of community responsibility for maintenance.

In response to this situation, Les suggested that we could drill small-diameter wells and install hand pumps near churches or other common public land. In this way, the entire community surrounding each well could safely draw water. Together, we surveyed a few of the sites he had in mind to start this "Village Water Well Strategy." By encouraging a sense of local ownership and developing local expertise through training, wells could be better maintained and communities could work together to share the benefits. He was concerned that the most difficult obstacle would be the Haitian mind-set of allowing "the white man" to do it. This attitude was created by well-meaning people who failed to include local villagers in the planning and implementation of the programs. Les convinced me that the local people needed to pay what they could afford in order to experience ownership of the wells. This strategy sparked my imagination, and it became the centerpiece for future projects. This Village Water Well Strategy served as the infrastructure for every Lifewater International project during the beginning of our ministry.

A VISION EMERGES

As I prepared for a comprehensive logical analysis of the Haiti Project challenges, the following list of assumptions took shape:

1. This project should function as a water development school to train local nationals.

2. Each local village would be empowered to take ownership of its well to keep it functional.

3. Where it was legal, well sites next to community centers (e.g., a church) would be targeted, so that the well would be seen as a source of public water.

4. How costs would be shared—such as time and dollars to train drilling crews and repair crews—would be computed before beginning any project.

5. We would estimate the amount of time required for a Lifewater team to complete a project and also what was needed for the local people to carry on independently.

6. Given the extreme poverty of those served, there would need to be a means of connecting U.S. donors with projects, to assist with the local community's contribution in the cost of construction and maintenance.

7. Health and hygiene education for local trainers would be necessary to optimize the benefits of safe water.

8. Lifewater would recruit a sufficient number of U.S. volunteers with the necessary technical experience and skills, as well as skills in cross-cultural communication.

9. Temporary strategies, such as using simple water filters, could provide transitional solutions to help save lives during the start-up phase of the project infrastructure.

With these assumptions in mind, the Village Water Well Strategy was born! The Haiti Project would be the prototype. I estimated that this first project would require two U.S.-based volunteers, one drilling machine, spare parts for repairs, funds for shipping, airfares, import fees, food, lodging and administration fees. I calculated the project would require a six-year process.

The first year would involve organizing the people involved, choosing the initial sites, identifying the equipment and then getting it on-site—shipping, clearing customs and transportation. From there we would drill the first demonstration well, construct the pump slab and install a hand pump. In the process, we would train a local crew. The second year would require the U.S. Lifewater trainers to return to the project for the next round of training to guide the new crew through the learning curve. This second phase of training would take place after the local crew had learned, through their mistakes and failures, how to identify problems before they occurred. Then the third, fourth and fifth years would require a decreasing scale of U.S. Lifewater subsidy and an increasing scale of local community support to ensure that the program would become self-sustaining by the sixth year. The local people would learn that while water from rivers, open pits and other potentially dangerous sources was free, safe water was not free. If our project was to succeed, the local people would need to learn to set aside some funds to keep the pumps operative and in good repair.

After creating several pages of spreadsheets and cost estimates, we concluded that the Haiti Project would cost approximately $30,000. Les and other Men for Missions donors paid for much of this early expense since Lifewater's meager funds were spread thin over projects developing elsewhere. We then divided this total cost by the estimated number of people who would be served with safe drinking water, and we were delighted to see that it would be a cash investment of only $3.60 per person! Given that a maintained well could easily last more than the average lifespan, we realized that this small investment could actually represent a lifetime supply and safe drinking water for the entire community. This seemed to be an amazing value since the United Nations Development Program at that time was projecting $15 to $40 per person for worldwide strategies being employed at the time.

HAITI'S VILLAGE WATER WELL STRATEGY BEGINS

Sometime after our return home, the first official project began when a young man named Chris Hill volunteered go to Haiti. Chris was a graduate of Azusa Pacific College (now Azusa Pacific University) and, like us, was member of Bethany Church of Sierra Madre. At that time I was teaching the college Sunday school class. In this class I would often use Lifewater experiences as examples of how the Christian life can be lived out in "word and deed." I sought to show the students how these two principles are inextricably linked, and I would often use Scripture passages to demonstrate how it is impossible to truly have one without the other.

Chris approached me after one class and explained that he'd felt challenged by my description of the Lifewater project being planned in Haiti. We arranged an evening together to talk and prayerfully decide if the Lord was calling him to this project. This meeting led to others that eventually focused on pragmatics, such as budgetary and scheduling issues. Then Chris and I met with Bethany Church's missions committee and received their approval to solicit funds from the members.

We began raising the needed funds. Chris visited several classes in our church, starting with his own college class, and many members responded generously. This was crucial because a project of this magnitude would not be inexpensive. The drill rig alone—a Deeprock S100 lightweight drilling machine—with necessary spare and replacement parts, freight, customs fees and surface transportation would cost approximately $12,000. Chris' Haiti airfare and his living expenses for three weeks would cost another $5,000. Les Babcock and several of the Men for Missions put up at least half of this amount. Thankfully, Lifewater had accrued a reserve of funds that could help. Because gifts had been designated "to be used where needed most," I was prepared to invest these funds in the Haiti project. After Chris invested a considerable amount of personal funds, the balance was provided by his friends and by Sunday school classes at Bethany. This was clearly a community effort!

TRAINING IN CAP-HAÏTIEN

Chris arrived in Port-au-Prince as Lorraine and I had months before and experienced the same bumpy journey to the OMS compound in Cap-Haïtien. This would be his residence for the next several weeks, and Les Babcock would be his overseer. Chris and Les discovered a young man named Ovil who became the first local national Lifewater trainee. The

OMS leadership, and particularly Les, would serve as the "action agency" in country. This model, Lifewater partnering with a local action agency to train local nationals, was the nucleus of Lifewater's mission strategy. Looking back, it is truly amazing to see that the core of Lifewater's mission and model has continued through all these years.

Les explained to Chris and Ovil how to locate suitable well locations in each village. He identified an area only a few miles from the OMS headquarters as the ideal place to begin. The three men traveled with their equipment to a spot that Les had visited many times before. This village was, unfortunately, a very typical example of village water health problems. But missionaries from OMS had previously established a church in this village, and Les strategically located the first well site near this church. A well at this spot would attract many villagers who had never before stepped inside the church. All those who visited the well while worship services were in process would also become familiar with the music of Haitian Christians praising Jesus. Though someone from the church kept track of how many new believers had made their first church visits as a result of the water well, I am happy the Lord is keeping the real record. Jesus' story about the sheep and the goats in Matthew 25 suggests that Christians help the poor without keeping a record of their good deeds.

This strategic well did bring many to the church. But, like the love of God, there were no strings attached. Through the years many people who did not enter the church also regularly used the well. Les Babcock was able to see firsthand that providing safe drinking water in this village—and many others like it—proved to unbelievers that Christians cared for them. To all of us involved with this work, the project exemplified the delight of a true "word and deed" endeavor.

During the three weeks that Chris was in Cap-Haïtien, Les Babcock, Ovil and he worked together to construct two or three wells. This modest beginning was a great encouragement, but it also demonstrated that the little S100 drill rig had very limited potential for worldwide use. Still, we learned a lot about our strategies and planning that, until then, had been untested. We now had a much better grasp of what such a project would involve in terms of people, time, dollars and equipment.

Other lessons were learned as well. First, we learned that showing people actual film footage of the work was a tremendous aid in delivering the Lifewater message back home in the United States. Chris had taken a video camera and recorded much of the work in progress as well as the completed wells. These early videos were great tools.

Chris also learned an interesting lesson one morning when he went out to the well site to begin installation of the hand pump. Looking into the well, he was surprised to see a frog looking back at him from the water! As a result, Chris learned the value of following the training manual, which stated that one should always leave the well covered securely!

The success of Lifewater projects has always hinged on the local nationals who are trained to carry on the work, and this early Haiti project was no exception. Fortunately such trainees are typically highly motivated and hardworking. Les Babcock's trainee Ovil was no exception. He was a bright young man and caught on quickly, learning how to use the drill, install the well casing, cement the surface pad, and install the hand pump. It was his job to recruit local people to begin pumping the muddy water out of the newly drilled well. This borehole cleanup process can often take two or three days. This much time is needed to get a well to settle down to a developed state, where the water enters the perforations and bottom slowly enough to no longer carry silt and sand but only clean, safe, cool water. Once this occurred, the entire community had access to lifesaving, healthy water. We knew that each well would be operated almost constantly, with little rest for the pump handle during daylight! Beginning in the morning hours and throughout the entire day, long lines would form with buckets placed in a row to indicate each person's position in the queue. This system worked quite well, and lines were seldom interrupted. The exception was when elderly folks would occasionally step in front as soon as they arrived because their age afforded them prestige in the community.

After Chris left, Les Babcock and Ovil continued the work. Les' dedication was matched by his initiative. After a short time, he was able to negotiate with the local USAID office, convincing them to provide free Mark II hand pumps for every well Lifewater would drill and complete. I am delighted to report that many of these pumps were still going strong over twenty years later.

THE FOLLOW-UP PHASE

Roughly two years later, Chris and I made a trip to follow up and document the progress of Lifewater's efforts in Haiti. The blessings of this second journey were deeply encouraging. It was a wonderful experience to hear Haitians express their joy regarding the water wells that were providing clean, safe water to their households. I brought my 35mm camera to document much of the progress that had occurred since the work had begun. These Haiti scenes became the core of my presentation whenever I was invited to tell the Lifewater story. The Holy Spirit used these early speaking events to touch the hearts of many. A good number of those who heard the story became strong supporters, and a few became regular donors who continue their support today.

I wish I could report that every project followed the above strategy to the letter. Not so! The Lord always has surprises to stretch our faith and to keep us alert for "it just so happened" events that are clearly divine directives. They remind us of God's voice, "Not by might nor by power, but by my Spirit" (Zechariah 4:6). In my experience, being patient and willing to make course corrections always brings greater honor to the name of Jesus.

Through the years, we welcomed new volunteers to Lifewater who were the result of OMS contacts. As our work in Haiti circulated through OMS newsletters read by other mission agencies, several became new action agencies with whom we started new projects.

Throughout the 1980s, Les Babcock served as our Lifewater field trainer in Haiti. We sent many volunteers to work in Haiti, and Les equipped them with the training they needed. My sons, Gene and Don, both served on one of these trips. By 1994 there were at least six different ongoing projects throughout Haiti. At the center of Lifewater's Haiti efforts was Les, who continued to faithfully give of his time and talents. As years rolled by, I longed to visit more frequently to see how the work was progressing.

CHAPTER 5
Our Early Years

World Vision was one of Lifewater's early partners. In 1980, I shared my ministry idea with them: a Christian organization composed of water resource management specialists ready to address the water needs of missionary agencies.

At the time, World Vision field offices were being approached by local people to help them resolve the major health problems in their villages that were being caused by contaminated water. Stories I read in many mission magazines convinced me that, as the requests arose, most agencies were selecting a person from their staff to operate as "the water specialist." This was an undue burden for one person. Only people in the field of water resource development understand how difficult that job would be! The resulting projects cost way too much for the quality of results achieved. We were interested in helping World Vision invest their money wisely as they responded to these village requests.

When I was finally able to meet the World Vision development director, I suggested to him that he offer me a current request coming from the field asking for help with some water problem. My approach was to take the request, analyze the need and determine how we at Lifewater could best resolve the issue. This Lifewater person would ask any additional questions from the requesting agency by direct correspondence and then design a project that would include the solution. We would aim for a financially conservative design solution that was most likely to succeed. We would also include solutions with alternative procedures incorporating more risk but costing less. Our proposal would include two or three more ways to address the problem.

World Vision asked us to review a request for a water development project they'd received from the Navajos. Water points on the reservation were far apart and very difficult for the people to use. Many Navajos traveled long distances in their pickup trucks to obtain a fifty-five-gallon drum of water, the safety of which was questionable, for a family's weekly supply. World Vision was asked to help with this potable water scarcity. The Navajo leaders requested a well next to a centrally located chapter house in order to supply water to anyone who came to fill their barrel. The World Vision executive was touched by the need and promised to do something for them.

After he visited the reservation, he asked me how I'd approach the project. I told him that to drill for water at this location in Hard Rock, Arizona, was very expensive because the water was contained in aquifers overlying geological formations that were very difficult to penetrate. I suggested they go to Colorado and hire a well driller to survey the area and offer an approximate cost. The company wouldn't be asked to bid on the job, but would only be paid to act as a consultant.

Several weeks later, instead of hiring the consultant, the executive invited me to visit the site and meet the missionary in charge of the Navajo Gospel Mission. Tom Dolaghan, the director of NGM and a missionary Bethany Church supported, was a personal friend. He and his wife, Betty, served the Navajos on their Arizona desert reservation to share the Christian gospel. I called Tom to tell him World Vision did not follow my suggestion to request a consulting company as an intermediate step but instead had asked me to come over with them to consult.

Mission Aviation Fellowship flew three of us from Lifewater to Hard Rock for a few days of meetings and field surveys. We discovered that drilling a well at that chapter house was going to be very expensive. For example, the Flagstaff Water Company had their new wells, in this type of geological formation, constructed by renting a drilling machine, putting a driller on their payroll and paying the bills until the well was complete. This information was discouraging to World Vision, the Navajo leaders and Tom Dolaghan. We were not sure how to fulfill the promise of help by World Vision.

Many groups had tried to help the Navajos with their difficult water conditions. We found seven very expensive Jensen Jack pumps on the reservation that had never been installed on wells. Someone knew the wells would be deep, so they bought the deep-well pumps before the wells were drilled. They probably launched into the project without realizing how much the wells would cost.

The government had just completed a two-thousand-foot well not far from the Navajo Gospel Mission compound. I proposed that, if it would be possible to get permission from the government, one of these deep-well Jack pumps might be put to use on it. Utilizing this existing well could be a quick solution to help World Vision honor its promise.

We also located an abandoned government well. The U.S. government experienced a cave-in during the drilling process and decided that the well casing would be too small for their use. I knew it could be used with a smaller casing and a Jack pump to provide a nice source of water. This plan was to be a stopgap to provide a source of good water quickly. Unfortunately, red tape and delays kept us from completing a functioning pump at this abandoned government well.

As the Lord would have it, on the last day of our visit our hosts took us to see a water well site the U.S. government had just completed. On the way I noticed a natural spring where Navajos were watering their sheep. I asked to stop and have a look. A shifted formation exposed a very weak aquifer spring that was seeping enough water to make a rancid, smelly puddle. Nobody had ever considered this type of a water site as a safe source. In my experience, horizontal well drilling was a construction technique employed to access water from aquifers in hardpan formations just like this one. The system keeps the water flowing through a horizontally constructed well, which protects it from surface contamination. I suggested we should explore this technique.

After discussing this matter with all the parties concerned, I offered to work up a cost estimate for a horizontal well drilling pilot project to reveal the feasibility of this method. An improved surface condition would be constructed with a sheep-watering tank so that the traditional use of these sources was not compromised. I did some research and, to my delight, discovered that the twenty-seven thousand square miles of Navajo reservation had sixty-seven of these water-seep sites, none of which had been developed into horizontal wells for human consumption. They were mostly being used to water the sheep.

I contacted A. W. Smith Horizontal Well Drilling Company, experts in the field. I prepared a budget of approximately $20,000, which included Mr. Smith delivering a horizontal well-drilling machine to the reservation, setting it up and drilling the first well while training a Lifewater volunteer. We all agreed on this plan. Upon completion of this horizontal well, World

Vision would purchase the machine and utilize Lifewater trainers to equip a Navajo crew for future well construction. The Navajo Gospel Mission would take possession of the machine and supervise the ongoing project.

World Vision wasn't convinced this strategy would work. I believed it would. I agreed to put up the initial funds with the proviso that if we produced a safe water well, World Vision would pay for this project and thus complete their promise and obligation to the Navajo leadership. Mr. Smith completed his assignment by constructing a successful well with a continuous flow that produced three gallons per minute. Then the machine was left in the possession of the Navajo Gospel Mission. Lifewater billed World Vision for the project and we were paid for it. I had high hopes we would work with them again.

Our first volunteer to participate in this training project, the one trained by Mr. Smith, was Mr. Tom Ennis. Tom worked on the reservation training a Navajo man named Arthur. Then Arthur drilled a few more on his own. I sent my two older sons, Gene and Don, to become familiar with this process and help with the construction of the next two or three wells, learning all the drilling skills from Arthur and Tom.

Don and Gene filmed the project, documenting the successful water provision and happy water users. Their video has some very dramatic footage of the drilling and completion of these horizontal wells. One completed well has a pipe sticking out of the side of a hillside. On the video, Don demonstrates the valve for an audience as it produces a steady stream of water, to flow twenty-four hours a day without any pump, just like a natural spring.

The Navajo Gospel Mission and tribe leadership were very pleased with the results.

Some months later, I attended a meeting with Tom Dolaghan at the Navajo Hard Rock headquarters. The wells were on the agenda. One of the Navajo leaders remarked to Tom how pleased he was that this Christian mission had supplied his people with the gift of safe water with no strings attached.

He even commented, "It was surprising to me that you are not requiring our people to come to your church or sing your songs in order to get this water supply. Thank you."

What a powerful moment. Tom had served the Navajos for years, with little return. He smiled the knowing smile of one who has "waited on the Lord." The objective of the water project had been achieved: proving to the Navajos that Christians really care.

In the end they chose to purchase three more horizontal well-drilling machines. These would have the capacity to develop the seventy-six sites on the Navajo reservation. NGM went on to use the same type of machine in Mexico, only this time they modified it to work as a vertical drilling machine, producing several successful wells. Tom shared with Lorraine and me that these projects were helping his mission agency demonstrate Christian love to the people they served.

OUR FIRST CONFERENCE FOR VOLUNTEERS

Attendees of our first volunteer conference in 1981 met at Bethany Church in Sierra Madre, California. Lorraine and I, together with two board members and four or five volunteers, continued to dream and plan ways to help the rural poor develop safe water supplies.

Our second annual volunteer conference took place in October of 1982, again at Bethany Church. Together we discussed the equipment and teaching strategies appropriate for the many new requesting agencies. Tim Cleath and Greg Hamer were our two best-qualified volunteers in attendance. We also planned who would receive a Lifewater project during the following year. There was a lot of controversy over the risks I was suggesting we would take by starting with equipment that would be inexpensive but within our budget. The machines we could afford would require us to take a calculated engineering risk with the elastic limits of drilling workloads. We knew the tasks placed on these machines would make them strain.

Our biggest strategy to save time and money would be shipping the equipment without first making a survey trip. Though this was against our better judgment, I was convinced that a thorough study of the applicants would yield good results. This benefit of saving one year would help us jump-start the ministry much sooner. In the end, the board agreed that this faster-start policy trumped all the negatives. In our first start-up years we continued to take this leapfrog time-saving approach. It was a catch-22 dilemma: in order to raise funds we needed to show successes; in order to show successes we needed funds. Thus we prayed, "Lord, You seem to work best when a project has meager funds but willing people. So we embark upon the unknown to serve people who are poor in Your name, since Your unseen footprints are leading us to go."

Since our ministry projects would be expensive, we needed to generate a larger donor base. At these volunteer conferences we were planning strategies that needed $20,000 to $30,000 and would take up to five years to accomplish. The ministry was "a school for nationals"—teaching local folks how to build and maintain their own wells. Our choice of tools to equip them would include those that might not last as long as their heavy-duty counterparts. But the cost savings made sense. This trade-off of light-duty equipment for economy was essential for our budget. We sought to be wise, knowing that in the future we'd need to afford heavier duty equipment. Larger would last longer but would still need to be within the means of repair and maintenance by a national team once they became independent of our training and support.

THE EARLY YEARS THROUGH 1990

My sister-in-law, Suzanne Pappas, was my secretary at Shaw Pump and Supply. She also took on the workload of the newly created Lifewater International ministry. She was especially efficient and prepared for the task. Like Lorraine and me, she'd become a Christian in her adult life. We had great talks together over issues that would arise in the course of our work and could spend entire coffee breaks discussing how the Holy Spirit was helping us to apply a passage of Scripture one of us had just read.

The United Nations designated 1981 to 1990 as the International Drinking Water Supply and Sanitation Decade to raise awareness about the need for clean water and sanitation. One hundred and twenty countries would meet at the UN building to plan strategies to bring safe water to two billion people. Dr. Peter Bourne was organizing the participants from the United States. I was invited to participate as the executive director of Lifewater International and observe the proceedings. It was a marvelous opportunity for us to make connections with many high officials in some of the countries we longed to serve. I relished the privilege of listening in on discussions about the most cost-effective and best strategies to accomplish the great task of bringing safe drinking water into many of the disadvantaged countries in the world.

In the late 1980s, a team from Mission Aviation Fellowship came to Lifewater to observe the S400 drilling machine. They had contracted us to purchase it and box it for their next flight to Irian Jaya (now Indonesia's West Papua province). The team from MAF included an engineer, Odo Siahaya. Not long after, Odo, who'd lived and served in Irian Jaya as a missionary, was sure the Holy Spirit was calling him to the Lifewater ministry. He convinced his superiors at Mission Aviation Fellowship to let him come to work at Lifewater and even to pay half of his salary. What a bargain and blessing for us! MAF shared in our beginnings by providing this support that finally allowed us to hire an engineer. Odo served as the team leader on several overseas trips that called for his skills. Since he is half Indonesian and half Dutch, his language skills and appearance allowed him to navigate many tight spots. Not looking like an average American was a definite asset to get through customs and government red tape!

Between Shaw Pump and Lifewater, the volume of work had become too much for Suzanne to manage alone. So Lorraine would come to work with me in the mornings and assist with the workload of both Shaw Pump and Lifewater. We were growing so rapidly that these two were very overworked and we discovered we needed a third person. At this period in our growth all salaries were being paid by Shaw Pump since Lifewater income was stretched just to cover overhead and project expenses.

The Lord brought us Allison Rowart to meet the need of this increased workload. The opportunity to use her skills as the third Lifewater employee was an opportunity for her to apply her Christian mission calling. Since Lifewater was a ministry of love supported by Shaw Pump employees, they understood that the wages were less than industry standards. It took people with a Christian desire and calling to serve Jesus in this "word and deed" ministry. With Allison's and Suzanne's efficiency, Lorraine was able to reduce her schedule to part time, allowing her to become my traveling partner on Lifewater project trips overseas.

In 1994, a physics professor at San Diego State University, Dr. David Frost, offered to help us build a web page attached to the university's homepage. The Internet had just begun to attract attention as a worldwide communication tool. As our ministry continued to grow, we needed another person in the office to manage the incoming mail and finance. Odo highly recommended Elizabeth Karatij, who joined us in the office to manage the phones, mail and correspondence. We were also expanding our presence on the Internet and developing a web-based database.

Two computer experts, receiving only part-time salaries, also joined the ministry. Ryan Root, a genius at writing computer code, used a database program to write software connecting all of our finances related to donors and volunteers. Lifewater was automated! Ryan and another new part-time computer whiz, Chris White, worked together on other projects I had in the works in the hope that new Internet companies I was developing would be income generators for Lifewater. One site we were developing was called Church Body Network. We had basic electronic information on over three hundred thousand churches and one million suppliers and services. The site visitor could click on an area code to bring up a church or a supplier.

Lifewater was going through some very rapid growth in all three areas of the ministry: the number of volunteers, the number of projects and the need for dollars to keep up with these opportunities. It seemed to me that the most likely place for us to grow the ministry financially was through large donations from foundations. My friends at church, although faithful supporters, would not be able to contribute anywhere close to the amount we would need to continue to grow our presence in the mission field. Soliciting funds from foundations would be a new challenge for me, so I had to learn a new skill. At the library I looked up names of Christian foundations supporting relief and development in poor rural areas of the world, identifying the ones that would consider water resource development.

OUR NEXT PHASE OF MINISTRY

At our 1990 volunteer conference, Harry Westmoreland and Randy Fain conceived one major advance in the type of equipment that would become the centerpiece of our ministry. We had struggled along with light-duty machinery for eight years. It was time to consider spending more for the equipment.

Randy and Harry got together after a long day of sessions planning projects. They were inspired to work on the rig design that would meet our new criteria of "better for not much more." They called me to their hotel room to show me their preliminary pencil drawings. Familiar with new inventions, I was worried with the number of changes they were making in the design of this lightweight drilling machine. The risk with so many changes was that, with so many possible contributing points, it would be difficult to trace problems and design flaws. There were about eight basic differences in this new LS100 design over the S100 Stover rig we'd been using. I had confidence in these two men who had far more expertise with drilling machines than I. We gave our approval for them to begin the construction of a prototype for future Lifewater projects, with the caveat that we could not make any promises about purchases. They proceeded at their own expense, driven by their joy of serving Jesus through Lifewater. Praise the Lord!

It was only a few months later when Harry invited me to come to Houston and watch him run this prototype LS100 drilling rig. We set it up outside his shop. He started the drill while I videotaped the process. It was an exciting moment because the machine seemed to work flawlessly. There were a few leaky seals, which Harry quickly remedied, and I contributed a minor suggestion to improve the fluid seal. We drilled holes through the quill seals so that the grease would be transmitted underneath the seal lips interfacing with the rotating steel. This seemed to help stop the leak and reduce the wear.

In Houston, where we were drilling, there is a heavy clay layer, which caused the loss of circulation. Harry knew just what to do. By raising and lowering the drill pipe he was able to free up a large "boot" of clay that was hanging up above the drill, choking off the flow of fluid. This sophisticated skill regarding well drilling is an art, not a science—something we always communicate to those we train. Harry had gained the experience that allowed him to know what to do by his years of operating drilling rigs. Could we count on newly trained national Lifewater crews to get out of this kind of trouble? Probably not, but the learning process would help them on the next well.

This kind of problem solving was part of the long-range strategy we'd need to teach national well-drilling crews who would face all kinds of surprises, failures and breakdowns. Helping them through this kind of discouragement, to persevere for the great reward of a lasting and permanent safe water supply for their communities, was worth the effort. Water development requires safety precautions, and national teams would learn that drilling wells is a dangerous and repair-intensive business. On top of these inherent difficulties and risks, our Lifewater volunteers also faced the natural challenges inherent in cross-cultural communications. Our long-range purpose was to help local teams "learn how to be teachers" because they would be the ones to carry on the process of training other crews in their countries.

LIFEWATER'S FIRST FULL-TIME EMPLOYEES

Our staff had become overloaded with requests for projects. I knew it was time to enlist some engineers and geologists from our crew of active volunteers to join us on staff. The first name the Lord brought to mind was Patricia Hettinger. She was serving with the state of Montana as a surface water hydrologist. She had been to a few Lifewater conferences and participated in project trips. I had observed her leadership skills and knew she would make a great new employee and ministry partner. The Lord urged me to give her a call to see if she might be interested in changing careers to become involved full time in Christian ministry. When I got her on the phone, she explained she had just completed a major project for Montana and it was the ideal time to consider my offer. After a brief discussion about a Lifewater salary, representing less than half of what she was making, she said she'd pack up her things and move to California to join us! Needless to say, I was thrilled that the Lord had called her away from a very fine career in the industry to become a missionary. Pat jumped right into organizing our overseas projects with spreadsheets and budgets. She was a critical addition to our staff for handling the exponential growth of Lifewater.

Not long after Pat joined us, but before Lifewater moved to San Luis Obispo, Fred Proby and his wife, Janet, were ready to come on board full time. Fred was being inspired by the Holy Spirit to step out of the business world and use his geology skills to help the poor by providing safe water wells. The

Lord had given him a vision to take a drill rig under one arm and a Bible under the other and go do "word and deed" projects in Africa in Jesus' name. When he visited my office one day to announce his plan, I told him it was wonderful to hear how another Christian committed to the Great Commission was so like-minded. We discussed our strategy at Lifewater, and he was convicted to follow the Lord's "footprints unseen" directly to the Lifewater office. We both knew this was a divine appointment.

Fred's main job was volunteer director, but he also was responsible for managing the website and identifying a partner to whom we could outsource our computer programming needs. Janet, who had a teaching credential, presented workshops at our annual conferences. She developed a particularly helpful presentation entitled Home Alone. This paper and discussion was very helpful for the spouses of volunteers going overseas on trips and leaving the family at home. Fred and his wife, Janet, became senior members on staff who were critical in shaping Lifewater's future.

The same year, I received a telephone call from John Nadolski in Wyoming. He had been to a Lifewater conference where he sensed that someday he would like to be on staff full time. When the Peabody Coal Mine offered him a wonderful retirement package, he asked me if there would be a possibility for him to join the staff. I'd observed John's leadership skills on projects and knew he was specially qualified because of his two degrees in geology and engineering. John and his wife, Marcia, had only one stipulation: "We do not want to live in a big city." I told them we were contemplating a move to San Luis Obispo County. I was just waiting for Lord to show us the place. In a few weeks we worked out the details, and he and his family were ready to move to California.

PART III

Lifewater Goes Global

CHAPTER 6
The Dominican Republic: The Hand Pump

Lifewater became aware that villagers all over the world faced difficulties with hand pumps. Most of these problems were associated with maintenance and repair. Many of the hand pumps being offered by commercial enterprises were complicated and required special roller bearings, gears or chains. These pieces were not something that most local village blacksmiths could repair or manufacture. Consequently, several institutions were working on how to improve the village hand pump to develop one that could be efficiently maintained by local workers. One such group was Georgia Tech University.

One day I received a telephone call from Jack Larson, who worked with Project Serve. Project Serve offered opportunities for high school students to visit the Dominican Republic and help construct cement-block churches over a three-week period. It was a wonderful experience for these teens to learn about the difficulties of life in poor rural villages. I'm sure it changed many young lives for the better.

Jack had identified several village areas where hand pumps were inoperative. Commercial pumps had been installed that required costly parts to repair. A valuable community resource was sitting idle for the lack of knowledge and parts to put these safe water sources back in operation. Villagers were often asking Jack if he could help them with this problem, and he assumed that it was a relatively simple matter. He recognized what a wonderful investment it would be to equip and train these villagers to be able to fix their pumps.

Jack found Lifewater in a missionary handbook of agencies helping missionaries resolve water problems in their communities. When he called me to tell me of this condition, I knew it was a fit for a Lifewater project. I was pleased to see what we could do to develop a partnership with him to assist these Dominican villagers.

At this time there was another missionary couple in the Dominican Republic who were familiar to Odo, our engineer. They'd offered us a place to stay if we would come down and help Jack. Odo and I contacted a Lifewater volunteer, Charles Purdel, who was willing to spend the time on this hand pump repair training project.

We would try to obtain the plans for these improved hand pumps being designed by Georgia Tech University. In the meantime, most of the pumps could be repaired with simple tools but expensive pump parts. This project would be a good value while we developed the village-level maintenance pump program for the Dominican Republic.

The project plan was to be developed by Odo and me as soon as funding was obtained through a major donor. In faith, we began the project using Lifewater's undesignated funds. Odo went down to the Dominican Republic, Charles Purdel met him there and for the next two weeks they trained a young man to be able to repair hand pumps in villages. The concepts about how to repair pumps were passed on, through him, to Dominican nationals. It was valuable training even if we would be unsuccessful in finding funds for the full range of the project.

When Odo returned, he and I strategized to develop pump parts that could be manufactured by local nationals, saving time and money in the repair of pump cylinders. These pump cylinders have plunger assemblies and seals, called cup leathers, which are often the main reason for pump failures. With my twenty-five years of experience at Shaw Pump, and with sales of many pump leathers and cylinders, I knew that a better product could be manufactured less expensively than the plunger cages that were being made out of cast bronze. There was also an additional expense for machining these bronze parts. Modern durable plastic could be a cost-saving answer.

I was familiar with modern injection molding that can produce durable plastic with the structural integrity and strength of bronze. So I designed a plunger cage assembly to be made from Celcon, a very strong and durable plastic. I made a drawing and a prototype from molding clay so that the injection-molding machinist could see the part in 3D. A shop in Alhambra agreed to produce the part for about $3,000.

In a few weeks, Odo and I were working on the first parts in our shop at Shaw Pump, trying to learn how to cut the threads with simple hand tools. It would be necessary for us to design the whole manufacturing system.

This system needed to include tools that could be replicated in rural poor villages. Odo took the lead and did a marvelous job producing the parts in a way that they could be duplicated in a simple shop overseas.

CHAPTER 7
Kenya: Our First Shop

It happened that we began our first pump shop in Kenya, not the Dominican Republic. We chose Kenya as our pilot project because we had excellent local management there. Unfortunately, the nationals we trained did not fully understand Odo when he told them how critical it was to take the proper steps in making the parts, to ensure the production of acceptable products. The tolerances, together with concentric threads, would be vital for a successful product. The first few parts the workers produced had threaded assemblies that were not concentric. When they were assembled, parts would work a few hours and then break. These early failures meant expensive labor problems each time the pumps had to be removed and repaired.

Odo and I had so much going on at Lifewater that we wouldn't be able to get to Kenya until the following year. What was most needed, to restore their confidence, was an immediate return trip. There was simply not enough manpower and dollars to help this crew get back on track. Once these workmen experienced failure it would be hard for them to regain confidence in the entire pump production shop.

This was a very frustrating experience. I knew that this single cage assembly, which could be produced in simple shops, would reduce the overall cost of a pump cylinder by about 30 percent. The call of higher-priority Lifewater projects would now cause this part and the family mold to sit on the shelf gathering dust. I was disappointed that this cottage industry, which can be so helpful to rural poor communities, would be one we were unable to implement.

The Lifewater ministry was growing at an extremely rapid pace in the late 1980s. It required us to make management decisions based on the "good steward" principle. That meant we would prioritize our most cost-effective training and equipping programs: our well-drilling programs and village water well pump repair projects.

These programs were achieving so much success that I reluctantly chose to postpone another wonderful cottage industry possibility. This time it was a system for making single-family safe water filters that involved a clay pot by Potters for Peace. These wonderful cottage industries had to be put on hold until we had sufficient volunteers and funding to make them successful. It was very frustrating to realize we simply did not have sufficient resources of personnel or dollars to do all the good things we knew were possible.

CHAPTER 8
Haiti: My Last Trip

In 2001, I planned a trip to review the performance of Lifewater projects in Haiti. I hoped to survey many of the projects that had been completed since my first visit there with Lorraine twenty years earlier. I had planned to take my dear friend and prayer partner, Jeff Bjorck, with me. He'd recently joined Lifewater's board and was excited about gleaning some firsthand experience. The board also felt it would be good for Dan Stevens, our new executive director, to accompany us and gain his first exposure to Lifewater in the field.

Our local contact met us at the airport in Port-au-Prince and shuttled us through the crowded, smelly, smoky streets to the One Mission Society compound. The country was again in turmoil over politics and the poverty that was a result of political and economic instability. Riots had erupted and people were burning piles of tires in the middle of the road to disrupt transportation. That night we could hear gunfire in the streets. On the day of our departure from Port-au-Prince the violence continued to escalate. Concerned about getting through the streets to the airport, we prayed for God's travel mercies. Even without the political friction in the air, road travel would still have been a tense experience. Our driver lurched through traffic, occasionally driving on the wrong side of the road, and skirted deep ditches by inches. In other words, he drove like everyone else!

About a mile from the airport we came upon a small riot that was being quelled by the police and the military. As we were passing by, Haitian army soldiers were bailing out of their truck just fifty yards away from our lane of traffic. They were wearing riot gear and carrying automatic rifles to tame the crowd. Another truck, equipped with a water cannon, sped right in front of us, red lights flashing, to get to the scene. We didn't stop to watch. Our driver knew that when one riot breaks out it's more than likely others will follow. In an effort to avoid places he knew were likely for trouble, he avoided all main streets and ferried us down narrow rough roads as we prayed our way on to the airport.

Soon after arriving at the airport, we boarded a Missionary Aviation Fellowship plane bound for the island of La Gonâve, off the coast of Port-au-Prince. Here, as in Port-au-Prince, we inspected the ongoing work of

Lifewater. A crew of local nationals had been trained during previous years, and now it was time to witness their efforts. We had accommodations at the island's best hotel, which made the worst hotel in the USA seem like a five-star establishment! The local team was extremely kind, however, and provided us with wonderful meals.

The crew was asking me about my grandson. "When is Ben coming back?" The local girls had their eyes fixed on this handsome, single young man! He'd traveled there two years earlier, with Troy and Trudy Harper, to develop the strategy for our La Gonâve project. Troy and Trudy were Lifewater staff members assigned to this new opportunity. They helped raise the funds, located a heavy-duty surplus army truck, purchased it and shipped it to the site. Because our time was very limited, we arose early in the morning to eat a quick breakfast and then depart in the crew's army truck. It was a heavy-duty machine able to crawl over the rocky roads that had steep turns and patches of vegetation. Wells on this island were few and far between. Throughout the day we visited several with pumps that had been damaged or needed repair.

At our third stop, we were evaluating what was needed to fix a damaged pump. Dan, Jeff and I sat on the ground, in the shade of the truck, while the crew analyzed the repair project. A very young mother with a naked two-year-old boy on her hip casually strolled up to us. Jeff reached out his hand in a friendly gesture to the little boy. The little boy stretched out his arms to Jeff. This young mother put her boy down in Jeff's lap. Jeff received him cautiously. The three of us were chatting casually when I noticed, behind Jeff's back, that this young mother had started down the path to the village. It was hard for me to believe what I was seeing, but quickly realized she was going to leave the boy with Jeff.

I turned to Jeff and said, "That girl has started down the path to her village, and if you don't do something quickly you're going to be the boy's father."

Jeff's eyes widened as he realized this was no joke. He jumped to his feet, carrying the boy down to the mother. He insisted, "No, no, this is your boy."

The young mother reluctantly reclaimed her son. It was difficult for us to fathom being as desperate as this girl was. Abject poverty twists people's unrealized hopes for a life that is not full of drudgery and despair.

During our tour of various wells on the island of La Gonâve, I observed several that had been put out of commission as a result of children dropping rocks in them. Some had stones that had completely filled the well. This usually happened during attempts to repair the hand pump by various well-meaning groups. When they'd remove the hand pump, bringing it to town for repairs, they'd neglect to cover the opening. Unfortunately, the musical sound of a rock rattling down a long pipe into the ground is irresistible to most young kids. Sadly, the adults didn't seem to realize the impact this would have on their well. With only a few stones, a well that initially cost as much as $20,000 to construct could be rendered useless in the space of a short time. Local crews didn't know how to salvage these wells. In the USA it would be easy to set up a big air compressor to blow all the rocks out. But no such process was available on the impoverished island.

From La Gonâve we flew in another MAF plane to Cap-Haïtien, where Lifewater's village water well strategy had been conceived twenty years earlier. I was excited to see Les Babcock, who'd agreed to meet us there, and I was eager to see the fruits of the past two decades. I also wanted Jeff and Dan to witness the impact of our efforts. We hoped to identify both positive and negative effects of those early projects and use this information to improve Lifewater's ongoing work.

After landing at the Cap-Haïtien airport, we visited the same OMS compound that I had visited almost fifteen years earlier. We enjoyed wonderful hospitality at the compound and shared delightful fellowship with seven other Christian workers there.

While in Cap-Haïtien, Les took us to visit Ovil, Lifewater's first trained Haitian national, who'd continued working with Les for all these years. Ovil told me how grateful he was to Lifewater, and he had good reason.

He pointed to his two daughters and said, "Drilling Lifewater wells helped me put them both through school." Then he pointed to his house and told us, "Lifewater employment helped me construct this home."

He took me to the backyard, where the original drilling rig lay in a heap, completely worn out. The Lord had held it together for a life well beyond what could be expected of the simple machine. I was deeply moved to see how God had multiplied our early efforts in this man's life. Before we left we said a prayer of thanksgiving together.

In the days that followed, Les, Dan, Jeff and I drove to many of the early well sites in the countryside outside Cap-Haïtien. This is where I got to see firsthand that those early pumps were still going strong. At each one, we stopped and interviewed the people who were using the well at the time and gathered statistics that would help us understand how to improve our cost-effectiveness. We also asked questions to help us find better ways to link the gospel, in people's hearts and minds, to the provision of safe water. In many places, we found pastors who explained to us a wonderful connection they'd been able to make between safe, life-giving physical water and Jesus' living water. All four of us were truly amazed to see how God had taken simple efforts and produced so many blessings. Based on our findings, Les Babcock and I enjoyed recounting the results we'd correctly anticipated and the things that we learned to change as a result of unanticipated obstacles. We were both confident that our water ministry was not by our might, or by strength, but certainly by God's grace and Spirit.

As we flew back to the United States, I thanked God that He'd blessed me with such a wonderful glimpse into the harvest of two decades. It was so rewarding to see how the original strategy for the Lifewater village water well had produced projects with powerful "word and deed" results. Dan and Jeff were also moved by their experiences and could appreciate the enduring impact of the many things we saw. The fruit we witnessed had been woven into a fabric of God's "unseen footprints" extending all the way back to the day that Dave Graffenberger visited our Sunday school class at Bethany Church. As I looked ahead, I thanked God that He would continue the work through others like Dan and Jeff, Lifewater's new executive director and new board member, who had both clearly caught the vision.

CHAPTER 9
Return to Kenya: A Student Named Paul

I met Paul Maina during a development team trip to Uganda when he was a young man preparing to come to the United States to study agronomy at Cal Poly in San Luis Obispo. We decided to begin a Lifewater program under his direction as a secondary agency to the company he would be starting, when he returned with his graduate degree, called Farming Systems Kenya. Paul and I kept in touch for the three years he was in school in the United States, becoming good friends. When he concluded school and was ready to return to Kenya, I helped him write the proposal to offer people in the United States the opportunity to invest in Farming Systems Kenya. We had a send-off banquet at Bethany Church, where he had the opportunity to make friends with all of my friends in the hope that some would become donors. Lifewater Kenya became a reality in the years to follow.

Lorraine's second Lifewater trip was our visit to Lifewater Kenya in 1989. After a long, tiring flight we arrived in Nairobi, cleared customs and found Paul's brother, David Maina, waiting for us at the curb with the company's beat-up, but reliable, Peugeot pickup truck. After a short stop for a meal we were on our way for a two-hour trip. For the last fifty miles we were driving in twilight on a dangerous two-lane highway where buses and semitrucks were whizzing past on the other side of the road. Large oncoming trucks would cause our Peugeot to sway as they passed. When we later learned that David needed eyeglasses, but couldn't afford them, we realized that the ride was more dangerous than we'd realized. I arranged for him to receive an eye exam and glasses that week. Though David's skillful driving played a part, arriving safely was the grace of the Holy Spirit. At times like these, when we were on kingdom business, our experiences of God's presence was affirmed in many ways.

David had been directing Lifewater Kenya for a few years when he began negotiating with the Macuria Women's Project (MWP) about a safe water supply for 157 families. A fifteen-horsepower, three-phase 380 V Reda submersible pump supplied the deep-well water system was a gift from Shaw Pump and Supply. It pumped sixty gallons per minute to a tank on the hill from a newly constructed water well. Lifewater would supply the equipment, but David was requiring MWP to pay for all the labor and transportation.

The morning after we arrived, David met us in the hotel dining room. We had breakfast together before our trip to the project completion celebration planned at the MWP community. Though it looked like a beautiful day in Kenya, with some gentle puffy clouds over the horizon, David knew there was a threat of rain. This meant the dirt roads would be muddy and slippery. Though the bald tires of the Peugeot were no match for these conditions, he didn't tell us about the potential for rain. Since the celebration had been planned for several months, he loaded us up in the car in faith that we would be able to go to the event and come back with God's protection.

It was a beautiful ride. After a three-hour drive, we pulled up to the facility where a dozen or more women were singing as they marched toward us in a slow dancing cadence. We stopped and got out of the car to honor their welcome. This was a celebratory greeting offered to honored guests on special occasions. We felt very honored and told them so. After all the hugs, smiles and exchange of greetings, the women and men joyfully took us to the site of the water well to see their prized possession. It was humming along, pumping cool, clear water that was filling their tank on the hill. We were delighted to know that Lifewater had brought such a wonderful gift to this community. For Lorraine, David, and me, it was payment enough to have "love's reward" from these brothers and sisters in Christ.

We returned to the meeting house and found a special chicken dinner with Ougali, a delightful white maize mush that is akin to our cream of wheat. The meal lasted over an hour, with speeches of thanksgiving from several of those in leadership, mostly women. David noticed a gentle rain was beginning to fall. As quickly as Kenyan politeness would allow, he extracted us from the gathering, got us in the Peugeot, and hurried down the dirt road toward the safe tarmac twenty miles away. The road, dry and dusty a few hours earlier, was moistened by the rain. David knew that if the rain got heavier, the road would become dangerously slippery for our bald-tire vehicle, so he wanted to return to the paved part of the road as quickly as possible before the hard rains began.

As we began our journey back, the three of us were singing and praising the Lord for the wonderful experience we shared at the celebration service. About halfway back to the blacktop road, though, the rain began hard enough to make the roads very slick. David's face revealed concern as he guided the steering wheel to keep us from sliding off the crowned road. It was a delicate balance between speed, swerving to miss the potholes and still maintaining control.

Eventually the rain let up a bit. Unfortunately, we hit a pothole, David swerved and we landed in a ditch! Thankfully we landed on our side of the road, rather than swerving into oncoming traffic. We jolted to a stop without damage to the car or us. David, profusely apologetic, looked very concerned. Yet Lorraine and I also noticed that he was buoyed by a deep trust in God that we would somehow manage and get home before dark.

With Lorraine behind the wheel, David and I tried to push the slick-wheeled car out of the ditch…with no success. After our attempt, David and I hopped out of the rain and back in the car. Though we hoped someone would stop and help, two or three big trucks roared by us. They were heading in the direction from which we'd come and didn't offer to stop and help. We were preparing to pray in earnest when all of a sudden, from behind us at some distance, a man on a tractor pulled out from behind the trees. The vehicle crawled onto the road and headed toward us. It was just like the Lord to answer before we asked. The tractor driver and David chatted in Swahili while Lorraine and I watched the two of them get the Peugeot back on the road. The three of us offered our grateful thanks to the farmer and, with nervous rejoicing and singing, we proceeded on our way, giving thanks to the Lord for the man's help. David wasn't sure who the farmer was who owned the tractor in that area. As we chugged home, we thought of the passage in Hebrews that mentions "entertaining angels unaware" (Hebrews 13:2). Could this have been an angel, with an angel tractor and an angel chain? Some would say this was just a coincidence. I say it was God's hand.

Although we thought that the danger had passed, the rain soon became even more intense. When we arrived back on the tarmac we continued to praise God that the scary part of the trip had passed and we'd be arriving home just before dark.

We spent the following day at the Kerenget Secondary School. It wasn't far from town but did require traveling down some very rough, rocky roads. There were several places that would be challenging for brand new off-road vehicles. David had us on a tight schedule to see projects that his team had implemented over the previous few years. When we arrived at the school on that wonderful sunny day, the Kerenget students, who represented the top 10 percent of all students academically, were all sitting in the outdoor bleachers. I was given the privilege of addressing this audience of bright young people. At these government schools many teachers were active Christians and presented the gospel to their students in the course of their studies throughout the year. I'd prepared my remarks knowing these two details about my audience. In my message, I challenged the students to be good stewards of their privilege by becoming community leaders who would give God the glory for the successes in their lives. Many, like Paul, had the potential to become agricultural researchers. Some of their discoveries could potentially bring great progress to Kenya.

At the conclusion of the ceremony, several students gathered around me to express their thanks for the new well.

I was delighted to hear them gush, "We give you many thanks that water is now close by. We do not have to walk long distances with buckets. We now have one and a half more hours to study each day!"

There were over 250 students at this school. It was very satisfying to learn how a $2,000 water well would provide all of the students with extra time to study. And, of course, there was also the health benefit it would bring! This cost-effective ministry gift is so practical and yet provides countless benefits and blessings.

The next day we had the joy of visiting a project at Njoro, at a school for children with disabilities. Lifewater Kenya and Lifewater International had provided a rainwater catchment system and storage tank for this facility. David was taking us there for another reception and celebration ceremony to dedicate the system and tank. This time we had paved roads all the way! Along the way it was fun to stop and bargain with the street merchants. We arrived in Njoro just before noon and conducted the celebration and dedication service outside, next to the tank. Mothers and fathers of the students with disabilities were all there to join in.

After this time of joyous celebration, they led us into the school's general meeting room. It could safely accommodate about thirty people, but on this day there were at least fifty, with another dozen or so peering through open windows. We were escorted to a small wooden table at the front of the room, neatly set for the three of us. Because we were considered their honored guests, they wanted to serve us their best. We had a scrawny, tough boiled chicken, along with Ougali and a few carrots and onions. They considered it a gourmet meal, and we appreciated it! The balance of those attending sat on the floor and ate off pieces of newspaper, without the chicken and vegetables. Most of these people were extremely poor since their meager incomes were sorely taxed by the expense of keeping their handicapped children maintained in this school.

As is always the case, they invited me to give a "speech." I always started with an explanation about Lifewater International. It was important to me for them to know that Lorraine and I were the visual representation of a few hundred volunteers and a couple of thousand donors.

I explained to them, "We are the visual link to you from these people who have given their time and money to accomplish this project." I continued, "We have many donors, but most give small gifts that allow us to do projects like this one."

I felt it was important for them to realize that there was a large body of loving Christian friends on the other side of the world who cared about their water challenges. The tank we'd just dedicated was an expression of love that was not in word only but in deed and truth (1 John 3:18). Lifewater is a holistic gospel program. We care about people's physical bodies as well as their eternal souls. Beside the basic human needs of life, everyone needs to hear that Jesus has the answers to life that bring grace and peace with God to all who believe.

After the celebration and meal, as the three of us started for the door, a press of people clamored to shake our hands and give us grateful hugs. The last person at the door was a small, gray-haired lady waiting to shake our hands. As she reached out her hand to shake mine, I noticed her skin was rough and her palms were cracked from working the soil. She was obviously a subsistence farmer. I found out later that she was a widow supporting a granddaughter at this school. She offered me some gracious words in Swahili. Though not fluent, I understood her meaning by the expression and tears on her face. I was overcome with emotion. As time seemed to stop, I felt frozen, knowing whatever I said in English she would not understand. I wanted to tell her how grateful I was for the privilege of sharing this gift of a water supply to improve the health and workload for the school she supported. I wanted to tell her that the gift of her grateful loving heart was infinitely more valuable than the gift of material things we had brought. Our gift to this school did not drain my savings account. I knew I would go home to a bed with sheets and pillows, a home with hot and cold running water at my fingertips. My entire house has running water that is safe to drink. I wanted to explain these things, but David was busy with other people and wasn't available to interpret for me. So the handshake had to suffice.

What great blessings many of us seem to take for granted! The stark reality of the huge disparity between the rich and the poor struck me profoundly during this trip.

BEYOND INSTALLATION

When we originally sent the pump and motor for this project, I knew the unreliable power supply we'd have to depend on would shorten the life of the pump's motor. So I'd sent a spare motor in anticipation of this need. Sure enough, David phoned me about three months later to say they had a failure of unknown cause that burned out the motor. They were grateful I'd sent a spare to prepare for this possibility. I just hadn't expected it so soon. After they reinstalled the motor, they reported the evidence of a burn hole in the side of the motor. I'd learned from experience about these failures. This cause of this motor burn was clear to me: it was a lightning strike. So we sent the pump installer lightning arresters to David. He installed them in the pumping plant panel to save the next motor from a similar fate.

David shared with me that the downtime worried the residents who'd started gardens and acquired new goats. All were dependent upon this one well and one pump. In America companies always have backup systems and spare parts to avoid this kind of potential tragedy. But our slim Lifewater budget couldn't afford to offer this community the funds necessary to drill another well and supply another pump. This was a reality the Kenyans had to face and manage themselves. They needed to learn that an entire community relying on a single source of supply was risky business. Lifewater Kenya and the MWP families learned that the cost of providing a community with water on a continuous safe basis costs more money for backup dependability. They needed a second source of water since their community would become so dependent upon a continuous water supply. They would be using this water to raise animals, grow crops and gardens, and have extra water for personal use. At Lifewater we learned to warn requesting agencies about this possible "one well" dependence type of trouble. In the future we would be careful about supplying a single large pump.

Few Americans, much less rural villagers, understand this long-range need to provide safe water in the community. That's why there are so many inoperative systems throughout Africa. Many well-intentioned outsiders quickly provided a village well and, naturally, people began to depend on it. But the original donors forgot to train the people about repair and maintenance. It requires patience and perseverance for Lifewater teams to communicate these issues to prospective donors since it drives up the cost. Most people just do not understand this need for reliability when dealing with the basic human need for safe water. Once people become accustomed to having an abundant supply of water, the consequences of losing it can be disastrous.

CHAPTER 10
Nigeria: Soap and Water

John Apeh, a Nigerian student, was attending Biola University when he attended a presentation I gave on community development in Dr. Peter Kurtz's classroom. He was due to graduate the next year and return to Nigeria, where he planned to start the Life Training Center. As we spoke after the lecture, beginning to dream of what might be possible in Nigeria, I noticed that John was a soft-spoken man who choose his words carefully. This gave me confidence that he would follow through with any project we started. As our friendship grew, he visited me several times at Lifewater headquarters to strategize how we might build a partnership between our two organizations and cultures to bring "word and deed" projects in support of the gospel to the people of Odu Ofugo, Nigeria.

After John's graduation and return to Nigeria, we kept in correspondence, planning the future date when we would begin a Lifewater project through his newly established organization. The Life Training Center was designed to train pastors in "word and deed" projects. The fact that the Center shared Lifewater's commitment to sharing the gospel of Jesus and putting flesh on the gospel by living out God's love made them a great partner for Lifewater.

One of the best types of assistance these pastors could couple with their ministry would be a project to develop safe drinking water supplies in areas where people suffered from severe health problems because of contaminated water. These water projects, as John and I had designed them, were going to help these young pastors with very limited incomes.

Lifewater was finally able to ship a portable well-drilling machine to LTC, which was in a remote part of the interior of Nigeria. It turned out to be a costly and long process, involving difficulties clearing customs, spanning almost a year. Finally, John was able to unpack the rig and carefully inventory the parts. With the exception of a few hats and t-shirts that customs officials had confiscated, the parts were all there.

Lorraine and I boarded a jet in Los Angeles with one hundred pounds of extra luggage. I was bringing last-minute electrical pump parts, a panel transformer, baking utensils and canned food. The airline clerk let us through without an extra baggage charge when we shared the purpose for the extra items. Thanks be to God!

The usual flight through London connected with a British Airways flight to Kano, Nigeria. We experienced delays and arrived in Nigeria at twilight instead of noon. Because the airport clearing center at Kano had no lights, the four lines of people waiting at customs to get passport clearance was sheer bedlam in the dark. A few Nigerian people, who'd known what to expect, had flashlights. The majority of passengers were Nigerians returning home who, like us, were most likely late and didn't want to travel the roads at night. So everybody was in a hurry, pushing and shoving.

We finally made it into the holding area. The customs officials wanted to open the boxes of additional things besides our luggage. One official was particularly intrigued by one box that was very heavy for its size. Bound up with strong nylon straps, it contained a large transformer to run the school's submersible pump. Without a tool to cut them, he tried to use his teeth to cut the straps and open the box. We told him what was inside, but he was insistent that he be able to look at the contents. After almost breaking his teeth, he gave up and believed us. The officials at this airport were not too friendly to Christians since Muslims dominated the area. After snickering and making fun of us, they discussed whether we'd be cleared. By this time John had arrived and made his way through the crowd to rescue us. Just in time! As a national, he knew how to negotiate with these fellows. After some haggling, he got them to agree to let us through, tax free.

We piled our luggage on a shopping cart, pushed our way through the crowds and reached John's waiting Peugeot. Paul Maliga, the chairman of the Life Training Center board, accompanied John. We set out for Paul's comfortable house, where we could recover from jet lag and prepare for the next day's journey south through Nigeria to John's compound at Odu Ofugo. John had us come through Kano because the airport closer to LTC was a much more difficult entry point through which to clear customs.

After leaving the crowded city of Kano, with its noisy traffic and smoky air, the highways turned into two-lane, heavily trafficked roads. They were typical African roads, with a variety of small and large potholes. Familiar with the journey ahead of us, John drove as fast as possible to get us to our destination before nightfall. People walking along the road, using it as a sidewalk, would be warned by the Peugeot horn well in advance of our passing. They would often step off the road just before we would whiz by. Trucks and buses coming the other way were traveling at unsafe speeds, and our car would swish and sway from the wind as they passed by. Even giving the road his full attention, John would occasionally hit a pothole that I thought would surely break a wheel off. But the car kept rolling. John told us a joke about African roads: If you ever see a man driving straight down an African road you know he's drunk.

John knew a quaint little place to eat something light about halfway through our journey. He assured us that the food would be safe for us to eat. Wary, Lorraine and I still chose menu items that were hot or were fruits that we could peel ourselves.

While traveling after our meal, we passed many vehicles that had been abandoned after accidents. White crosses along the side of the road designated those who had lost their life in these wrecks. By late afternoon we were passing the large steel mill at Lukoja. This meant we were only two hours from the compound. The sun began to set, making visibility difficult. Unfortunately, John didn't see a large tree stump and branches in the road and we hit them, full on! It forced us to swerve and almost tip over. As we slowed to a stop beside the road, John was afraid the car was damaged. Pulling some branches from the wheel well on the right front side, though, allowed the car to roll smoothly again.

We worried about whether or not to drive the car again. We had another twenty minutes to go, and John did not want us to spend the night on the road where bandits often robbed people, or worse, after dark. We got back in the car and John started the engine. He put it in gear and began to roll forward. Except for some squeaks, it seemed to be okay. John started going a little faster until he felt secure that it was going to drive well. The front wheels were out of alignment, but not enough to keep us from proceeding. When we finally rolled into the compound, John was praising the Lord. We joined in but didn't understand what John did about the dangers the Lord kept us from by holding that car together until we arrived.

On the twenty-acre compound of the Life Training Center, John's team had constructed a number of buildings: a central conference room, a series of eight classrooms, a series of twelve student bedrooms, the director's home and the missionary guesthouse where Lorraine and I stayed.

During the two weeks Lorraine and I stayed at his compound, John and I developed detailed plans for Lifewater crew training. I worked up schedules to help two crews of three people each learn the basics of the drilling machine in this brief time. At that time in our ministry, we did not have enough trained volunteers who were able to stay for a full training period of time, so I chose to take the risk of spending only one week demonstrating the drilling machine to these new crews. They had accrued school classroom time and had plenty of property on the compound to practice.

The first morning after we'd arrived, we arose to see many Nigerian children whose faces were pressed up to the windows of the guesthouse to look at the strange white people. We were in a real fishbowl. Fortunately, the bathroom served as a dressing room since the windows were too high for people outside to peer through. One of the workers came by to give us fresh bananas and eggs. As he approached our porch, he killed a large black scorpion. Later in the day, while I was filming John giving a tour around the compound, we paused to take a picture of this big scorpion. John passed it off with a chuckle as he playfully explained to the camera, "Stopped this creature from stinging us to death!"

John and I planned to gather all of the participants in the conference center for a round of introductions. We used the time to give a description of what would take place during the following days. We were launching a partnership and long-range community development plan that was quite ambitious.

Starting that afternoon, six eager young men gathered up the drill machine accessories and carried them to a site on the campus where I would begin the process. I would be showing these men how to dig the mud pits and demonstrating the machine for the first time. We'd just completed a few hours of introductions in a classroom setting explaining well drilling and groundwater usage. This entire training effort was very short and would leave a lot for the crew to discover on their own from the information I was leaving with them. Much of the skill they'd need would come from practical work experience. They would make errors of judgment in drilling wells and learn, like most people do, the hard way. Even with weeks or months of training, new crews still make mistakes.

In a few hours they had assembled the machine and dug the mud pits. Everybody was eager to fire up the drilling machine and mud pump to begin the process. I explained that there would be a very orderly chain of events that would take place before this start-up could happen. If the steps were performed out of order, everybody would get wet with muddy water. With great delight the moment came when we fired up the mud pump, got the fluid circulating, started up the drill, opened the valve and watched the mud come out of the drill stem while the drill operator began cranking the drill bit into the earth. The crew was delighted. After one drill stem I made them stop and shut everything down to review all the tasks that the operators needed to perform in harmony to construct a well using this machine.

A year later, I learned that the program had stopped because the crew got the drill stem stuck in a well when they'd lost circulation. It was a common drilling error made frequently by trainees. Thankfully John knew it wouldn't be long before the crew would be going again and the machine would be functional. Lifewater would send two more volunteer trainers back to the site to get them going again, but it wouldn't be until two years later.

The next day at the center, the men and women were eager to learn about more potential "word and deed" projects for their community development programs. They took notes as we laid out charts and graphs of programs and time frames. The fund-raising abilities of the Lifewater staff were dependent upon our small mailing list, and this was going to be the largest project we'd ever attempted. John had developed his own list of donors from speaking engagements he had in the United States before he left for Nigeria. He gave me this list and, together with the Lifewater donors, we hoped to be able to raise the funds we needed to finish the Life Training Center and fund the village water well drilling program.

During the trip Lorraine was busy participating with the LTC women's group. She had brought all of the pots and pans and implements necessary to make soap and planned to leave them with the women's center. The project would be a means for some of them to make a small wage while contributing to this essential hygiene program for the community. One obstacle the women faced was finding enough animal fat to make the soap.

We hadn't predicted that they wouldn't have extra fat for soap because it was too valuable as food. John was gracious enough to gather some so Lorraine could demonstrate the process to the ladies should they ever have the luxury of enough fat to make soap.

When the soap making wasn't successful, the ladies were eager to learn how to make bread. The baking event would take place at a nearby technical school with seventy young ladies. Lorraine had brought several recipes. One was banana bread. The people had plenty of bananas, but had never thought of using them as an ingredient in bread. The first loaves were baked in an oven whose door wouldn't fully close, so Lorraine had to guess at temperatures. She did a great job because the bread came out perfectly. The ladies reported the next day that the banana bread made a big hit with their husbands and family. They all treated it like cake. The ladies were delighted to learn a simple process of using local resources to bring this new joy into their homes.

When it was time to return home, we set out toward the airport in the trusty Peugeot. This time it wasn't so trusty. A few blocks from the airport it coughed, sputtered and died. John opened the hood, analyzed the problem and got under the vehicle to remove a gas line that he believed to be the cause of our problem. Lorraine and I were sitting in the back seat praying for him. I remember he put his mouth over the gas line tube, drew hard and unplugged the line, getting a mouthful of gasoline. Not a very good experience. He quickly washed his mouth with water but the terrible odor and taste did not dilute very much. John assembled the tubing to the tank once again and got back in the car. It started as soon as the line cleared the air. Because we'd broken down in a questionable area, where several threatening-looking men kept staring at us, we were very relieved to get the car rolling again and finally arrive at the airport curb. John parked the car, and the three of us dragged our luggage to the British Airways counter to check in. We said our good-byes to John with a tearful expression of Christian joy and love, wondering if we would ever see each other again.

We walked through the security doors to submit to a search by Nigerian officials looking for contraband. When they looked through my carry-on bag and discovered my medicines, they found it very unusual for somebody to be taking so many medicines. They questioned me about the contents, and when I explained and reassured them, they were satisfied. One fellow picked up my underarm deodorant. He took off the top and smelled it. He looked at the other custom officers and snickered, implying that it was pretty strange of me to want this odor on my body. Because most Nigerians bathed in questionable water, often without soap, body odor was commonplace. The smell was pervasive wherever large groups of people gathered.

Lorraine and I were so pleased to get back to our beds with clean sheets, warm and hot taps in our shower, and a pantry full of familiar foods. It is always such a sobering experience to return home to such abundant blessings most of us take for granted.

CHAPTER 11
North Africa: Gaining Access to a Closed Country

In the middle of the 1980s, a young water engineer wrote to us explaining how he planned to be a team member with Frontiers in North Africa. Many parts of North Africa are desert areas where water is hard to come by, and he'd become aware of the need for safe water in villages in several remote areas.

At the outset it looked like it would be a long, slow effort. There were many departments from which to obtain approvals, and each required the completion of many forms. The process required connecting frequently by letter or telephone. More than three years later, we'd finalized almost all of the papers with the government. But at that point, the engineer from Frontiers became discouraged and returned to the United States. He sent us a large envelope of documents and correspondence representing all he'd accomplished. The packet of information revealed that he was being shuffled from one agency to another, and it appeared as if they just didn't care if he ever got approval. Because we had no one else who wanted to pick up the mantle, the information was stored in a blue binder, where it would wait for the "unseen footprints" of God to guide us when the time was right.

That leading unfolded in a way we didn't expect. Six years after the North Africa project had begun, I was invited to give a Lifewater presentation at a Christian relief and development conference in Santa Fe, New Mexico. There, I met a man named Scott, the Spanish director of another Christian community development agency. He was very interested in our history in North Africa. After my brief presentation this young director approached me and explained his agency's dilemma concerning a couple from Central America who'd recently been called to live out the gospel by serving in North Africa. Rodrigo was a water engineer by profession who was trying to fit into North African society by developing a leather goods import-export business. He and his wife were somewhat discouraged since they'd not yet discovered what they believed to be God's ultimate purpose for them in North Africa. We were both delighted that "it just so happened" the Lord had brought us together. We shared stories and strategies about how we might help Rodrigo transition from working as a leather merchant to using his highest calling as a water engineer.

We initiated correspondence with Rodrigo by sending him the package of information developed by the Frontiers engineer. This began the laborious process of reestablishing our effort to obtain legal government recognition. Eighteen months later Rodrigo called me to say that the papers and documents were ready to sign, but the government wanted the director of Lifewater to come there for the signing.

"Me?" I clarified, "Go to North Africa? Wow, I don't know."

After a few days of prayer with staff and family, I decided to go.

I was able to obtain a very reasonable airfare connecting through Malaga, Spain. The Spanish agency who'd sent Rodrigo had a wonderful guesthouse there overlooking the Mediterranean Sea. It was in an elegant hillside community with wonderful balmy weather. I recovered from jet lag in one day and was ready to take the flight to North Africa.

Upon arrival in Africa, I handed the immigration officer our correspondence from the director of North Africa's Department of the Interior. He briefly perused it, as if reading it thoroughly. Then he handed it back to me and stamped my passport. When I brought my luggage out through the clearing areas to the curbside traffic, Rodrigo was waiting for me.

We had never met, so he was holding up a sign that read "Lifewater." This was a relief to me since I was in a foreign Muslim country with signs I couldn't read and very few English-speaking people. Rodrigo knew just enough English to get me in his car and head toward his home in a city two hours from the airport. When we arrived, his wife, Sofia, greeted me with a big grin and enough English words to reassure me we would be able to communicate adequately. This couple spoke Spanish, French, some English, and were learning North African Arabic. What dedication to a calling!

That evening we had a great time sharing our experiences about meeting Christ and the Christian life into which He'd invited us. Like the engineer he was, Rodrigo had the details of my ten-day visit well organized.

We spent the first day after my arrival visiting government offices and being introduced to the people with whom he'd been negotiating in order to establish Lifewater-North Africa.

Rodrigo had recently purchased a small automobile from a Brazilian foreign diplomat who was leaving the country. During my visit, Rodrigo had not yet changed the license plates that were a special blue color, designating a foreign ambassador. We had fun driving through town when the police would offer us the right of way when it was not really our turn to go first! We looked the perfect pair. Rodrigo, being a Central American, looked like an Arab. To enhance his appearance as a local, he had grown a mustache. I was a considerably larger man, white-skinned and gray-hair. Seated in the passenger seat, it appeared that I must have been the diplomat! At the government buildings where parking was scarce, we drove right up to the front doors and parked anywhere there was space enough for the little car, whether or not there were white lines indicating a parking space. What fun!

The following day we met with the director of the Bureau of Land Management. He was the top person we needed to sign our papers and give us permission to begin the safe water relief and development projects for the Berbers of North Africa. These descendants of the pre-Arab inhabitants of North Africa were scattered across a number of North African regions. Rodrigo had discovered they were in desperate need of our services. Any existing wells were highly contaminated because they did not have covers. These water points needed a constructed concrete cover to complete the community wells for lasting and sustainable public use. Since people had no alternative, they were using the water and suffered repeated waterborne illnesses.

We met with the director in his large, mahogany-paneled office with comfortable leather-cushioned chairs. In the waiting room the very efficient male secretary asked our names, took our business cards and asked us to be seated, disappearing back into the director's office. This director was very busy, or at least appeared to be, but about thirty minutes later we were called into his office. This was Rodrigo's first meeting with him. Without me, the director of Lifewater, he would never have received the appointment. The government probably never expected that the Lifewater director would come to North Africa to sign the papers, especially for the purpose of helping the Berbers with their safe water needs as a nonprofit.

It was apparent from our conversation that this puzzled the director. He was intrigued by what we were up to. The government knew we were a team of Christian engineers, and we knew they'd monitor our activities to see if we'd try to convert Muslims and Berbers to become Christians. Though he didn't express this in the meeting, Rodrigo and I both understood the government's interests.

After the niceties of introduction and a cup of tea, he asked Rodrigo for the specific plans for his water development project. They began speaking in Arabic, but when Rodrigo told him he was just learning the language, they switched to French and communicated rapidly. I sat there like a bump on a log until the director turned to me and asked in perfect English, "And why have you chosen to come to this country to set up Lifewater?"

As I'd been praying about our work in North Africa, the Holy Spirit had made me aware that this kind of question would be asked of me in a quick surprise manner, just as it was. I suspect the director thought that if he caught me unaware, he could discern whether I had some secret agenda.

I began, "I'm in the water business in America and the Lord has been very good to me. So I'm wanting to give back to people with special water needs from my experience and resources."

He interrupted and said, "Very well."

Then he turned to Rodrigo and spoke again in French. I learned later that Rodrigo was requesting permission to build the first well. As they spoke, this director became quite agitated that Rodrigo would come into his office and ask for permission to retrofit one well in the Suza community of Sovabot.

He said, "One well!" in English, for my benefit, to underscore the offense of wasting his valuable time over such a trivial matter.

Rodrigo quickly explained that this was just the pilot project for beginning many community wells.

After hearing the larger strategy, the director calmed down and decided we were most likely a legitimate organization. He finally agreed, in English, "Okay, you have my approval."

Rodrigo returned to speaking French and explained to him that we needed a letter from him confirming this approval.

The director assured him, "This is a free country, go ahead. You don't need a letter from me."

Rodrigo continued to press the issue until the director finally said, "All right, I'll give you a letter. Come back tomorrow."

The director stepped on the foot pedal under his desk and a sharp young man in a white shirt and black tie walked up to his desk prepared with a notepad. The director told him to prepare a letter for us explaining of his approval for Lifewater projects. He invited us to come back the following day to receive the letter and government papers of approval we had been waiting for seven years to obtain.

We returned home in our diplomatic car singing and praising the Lord for this wonderful opening. Rodrigo understood government politics. He explained to me how no bureau chief wants to give permission for anything for fear of his superior's objection and displeasure. This letter, though, was coming from the highest official and would open every door. As it turned out, it did!

The next day we returned to the government office, where we waited in the lobby for thirty minutes. The secretary came out and said, "I'm sorry the letter is not prepared, please come back tomorrow."

After one more "tomorrow," on the third day, the secretary instructed us to wait in the lobby while he typed the letter. Then he took it to the director for his signature. Thirty minutes later, Rodrigo had his letter in hand and the Lifewater-North Africa ministry began!

The timing was perfect. The Lord knew we would have three days of delays at the government offices. Rodrigo was scheduled to go to Suza the next day for a series of activities he'd previously planned. On our way, we picked up another member of Rodrigo's team who spoke Arabic and would help us with translation. Our trip to Suza was a full day's journey to the high desert country where most of the communities were very poor. It was also an area where most of the people have never heard the name of Jesus. It seemed like the government despised the Berbers because they weren't Muslim. They were considered outcasts.

In this area the government had constructed community wells that were six feet in diameter and 90 to 120 feet deep. For some reason, the government left these wells open at the top with no apparatus to access the water deep in these wells. The Berbers were left to fend for themselves with ropes and buckets. It seemed the government had run out of funds to complete the wells. I suspect that if the right people in the government knew this condition existed, there would have been a project to complete the wells sooner. But the Berbers received notice of delay after delay. It was counterproductive for community health since, with children throwing garbage and other items into the wells, they were sure to become contaminated. We also heard a tragic story about a child who fell in and died. His death raised the level of community protest to the government, but nothing was done to keep this from happening again.

Rodrigo's dream to bring the blessing of safe water to these people had been born when he'd learned of these difficult circumstances. Constructing a concrete cover on the ground next to the well was doable: Ten men could lift the concrete cover off the ground and up to the well rim. Rodrigo's design allowed for a hole in the center from which to lower a cylinder pump on pipe to the bottom. A hand pump at the surface would allow everybody to have safe water to drink from an aquifer that would finally be sealed off from contamination.

We spent our first night in Suza at a ten-room local hotel. Each of the three of us—Rodrigo, myself and the translator—had an individual room. The accommodations were especially comfortable for a developing nation. When I explained to the hotel clerk that I snored loudly, he laughed. In his culture sleeping in a big room with lots of snoring people wasn't unusual.

The next morning we enjoyed a wonderful breakfast at the hotel and set out for an hour-long journey to Novabot. This would be the first village to receive Lifewater's help. As we drove off the main highway and into the community, we spotted the first well. It was close to the one-lane blacktop road. Two women with donkeys were drawing water from the well and loading containers on each donkey. Our interpreter explained to us that their culture didn't allow strange men to associate with local women at the well. He got out first, stood at some distance and explained to them who we were and what we were doing.

They were chatting when a gentleman appeared from behind a mound of earth, asking about our purpose. Our interpreter hit it off well with the man and beckoned us to come out of the car. The women seemed nervous about our presence, but the Berber gentleman put them at ease. I asked permission to take some pictures and he agreed. After taking some pictures, we returned to the car.

Instead of the three of us, though, there were now four of us inside!

As we drove down the road, Rodrigo asked in English, "What is he doing in our car?"

The interpreter answered with a smile on his face, "I don't know!"

Because we didn't have big concerns, we proceeded on. A few minutes later this stranger pointed out another well and we stopped to observe and take pictures. In this area villages were often spaced ten or twenty miles apart. After our stop we continued on to the community at Novabot, our ultimate destination, via several more miles of gravel roads and thirty more minutes of driving.

Rodrigo had visited before and observed the distress of the community from the contaminated water sources. He promised them he would attempt to get government permission to help them clean up the "one well" and put it in proper working order with a cement cover and hand pump. But when these Berbers had received offers of help before, those benefactors didn't accomplish anything, leaving the community disappointed. Faces filled with delight and joy when the Berbers saw Rodrigo returning as he'd promised!

We were invited to the home of the headman—who functions like a chief or mayor of a community—for a meeting. Because the room was full, we weren't sure which man was the headman. The meeting lasted an hour, and we were served sweet Fesery tea and biscuits, also known as cookies. The interpreter explained our program, including what plans were developing, and Rodrigo narrated what was expected of the community in terms of construction help, when he returned to supervise the work, and materials.

After the meeting we all walked down the canyon toward the well that was to receive the Lifewater retrofit system Rodrigo had designed. As we walked, many people began following us until there was quite a crowd. They seemed to come from nowhere. The villagers had noticed the automobile dust and had gathered at the place it was parked to see what was going on. I had fun snapping pictures of smiling faces. At the well site the odor emanating from the well revealed that it was contaminated. The stench was terrible, but this was the only water the community had for survival.

It would take a crew with lots of buckets and chlorine a day or two to muck it all out. Rodrigo and the interpreter explained to the community present what type of work and materials would be needed. They all smiled in agreement, eager to participate in this dire need for the community. Then we returned to the headman's house for a meal. A very colorful rug covered the dirt floor in the main room, about fifteen feet by fifteen feet, with three small windows near the ceiling. This space served as an all-purpose room. It was a wonderful meal of chicken and couscous, ending with some sort of sweet dessert. The meal took an hour, and friendly conversation followed.

At one point the interpreter told me that the people gathered were interested in why I was there and why I agreed to bring help from America. It was my delight to give my story about how the Lord Jesus Christ had blessed me. I did the best I could to make my testimony simple, including a brief description of my conversion at age twenty-five. Thankfully, the interpreter knew how to explain who this Jesus was and what He had done for me.

Later on that evening the interpreter explained what a wonderful opportunity it had been for him to explain about Jesus without risking the consequences he might suffer for trying to "convert" people. Those gathered had asked for the story, and they were my words and not his! If this "religious" conversation got back to any antagonistic North African official, he'd be hard-pressed to blame the interpreter.

After I completed my testimony, the stranger who'd joined us in our car at the first well began to speak, signaling his approval. As he spoke, the interpreter discovered he was the headman for the village!

On the way home we stopped at one of the ancient cities in North Africa. We walked the narrow streets that have been unchanged for more than two thousand years. The merchants were all eager to sell us their wares.

Back at Rodrigo's home the next evening, two days before I was to return to America, we drew construction plans and a pump design on a big piece of paper. I was familiar with the Zimbabwe Bush Pump and explained to Rodrigo about its construction and unique design that was so well suited for village repair and maintenance. He caught on immediately and confirmed that he would be able to get these pumps manufactured locally.

Over the years he has modified the design to make it even more sustainable by each local community. From the success of retrofitting a few wells in the Berber Suza area, Rodrigo's team was invited to bring some nurses into the community and explain about public health, hygiene and nutrition. The team has had wonderful success showing the love of Jesus Christ through these projects, without religious strings attached. The last word I received from this Lifewater team was that there were ten to fifteen people serving North Africans in Jesus' love.

CHAPTER 12
Philippines: "The Babies Don't Die Anymore"

In the early 1990s, our small staff and volunteers were being overwhelmed by requests for assistance with water resource development. Consequently, we weren't advertising. The single exception was *U.S. Water News*. The editor, Tom Bell, was a fine Christian man who was also a hydrogeologist. He was running a free ad for us. Our lack of any additional advertising caused some to call us the most obscure ministry in all of Christendom.

The 700 Club, a television program of the Christian Broadcasting Network, had been broadcasting about Operation Blessing, the network's charity meant to demonstrate God's love by alleviating human need and suffering around the world. Pastor John James, from Manila, called Operation Blessing to find help for many communities who were facing water contamination. People in those communities had already been writing in to Operation Blessing for assistance.

After the home office at Operation Blessing spoke to Pastor James, they called us. In addition to those who'd written them, their radio broadcasting had elicited a half dozen mission agencies pleading for help. The most urgent need was to eliminate contaminated water and the resulting waterborne diseases. It seemed like a wonderful opportunity to put an expert water well driller to work, ministering in his training capacity, with several agencies. It would raise our visibility among agencies with whom we desired to partner and would produce cost and ministry effectiveness.

I called Randy Fain, a Lifewater volunteer in Southern California who grew up in the well-drilling business. He had a robust pump and repair business in Escondido. Randy had expressed to me his desire to serve the Lord with his skills to help the poor in Jesus' name. He knew this type of work was labor intensive and often dangerous, but after consultation with his wife and scheduling his father to fill in for him while he was away, he told me he was ready to go.

Fortunately for Lifewater and our meager budget, Operation Blessing (OB) agreed to cover most of the expenses. Anxious to document the entire effort, OB planned to film our every action. The film crew planned to arrive in the Philippines after Lifewater had sent the three drilling rigs and pump supplies. The three agencies OB had offered to serve, by implementing a Lifewater program in their communities, were anxious to begin.

For our first trip, we arranged round-trip flights for Randy and me on Philippine Airlines for $900, a real bargain in those days. Once we landed we cleared customs, found Pastor James and headed off to the guesthouse. For our inaugural visit, John had arranged a series of meetings for us to explain our project strategy, timings and budget to the partner agencies.

During that first trip Randy and I were able to see a few sites on the island of Luzon, the largest island in the Philippines. The poverty so many people endured touched our hearts profoundly. Randy and I carefully chose all of the equipment, tools, repairs and supplies he would need for this first training program.

Our return trip to the Philippines took place about nine months later. The schedule and program were laid out as well as human planning allowed. The day after we landed, Randy and I began to unpack the shipment that had preceded our arrival. Unfortunately, there was a snafu with the support drilling legs of the Stover S100 machines. Randy quickly identified the problem and started contracting with local machine and welding shops to rectify the error. In the meantime, I took a bus journey up the main highway, to a town called Bang Bong, where the people were experiencing difficult iron contamination problems.

The bus ride was the most memorable experience for me. The bus had been built in the 1940s and was still running with old World War II tires and a diesel engine. The bus was the only way for me to make the trip without a very expensive passenger car ride. When I got on the bus, crammed full of people with sacks of grain in the aisles and chickens in cages, there was only one seat left. Since the people push and shove at the door to get the best seats, I tried to wait patiently to get on. I quickly learned what a bad idea that was. Since the only available seat was next to the vertical exhaust pipe, situated directly outside the body of the bus, with only the thin metal shell of the bus between us, the metal radiated heat for the whole trip. Needless to say, it was very uncomfortable. Throughout the trip, two or three gruff-looking men glanced my way quite often. I suspected they were planning to mug me if they got the chance. I thank the Lord and his angels who kept me safe.

The community of Bang Bong was suffering from inoperative wells and highly iron-mineralized water. I met with the local people to explain their options. Unfortunately, there weren't good solutions to change the mineralized water. Repairing the pumps, however, was a simple matter and they caught on quickly, learning how to replace the cup leathers and restore hand pumps to working order.

Returning to Bang Bong the next day meant another transportation adventure. The crowded old bus was again full of people and belongings, but this time I got a seat away from the exhaust pipe! The bus would travel at about sixty miles per hour down the tarmac, riddled with potholes, swaying back and forth as the driver made every attempt to avoid the bumps. The real danger, in my mind, was the narrow two-lane highway. Buses and semis traveling in opposite directions passed each other so closely that the wind shear and compression would cause the bus to sway so much that I thought it would crash. The Lord was with me and again, at the end of the day, I arrived safely at the guesthouse.

The next day, Randy's repaired rig was scheduled to begin drilling a water well at Tambotine. This community of seven thousand people was packed into five acres. Plywood shacks were constructed two stories high with small paths running between the structures. When we arrived to survey the site, one of the local leaders met us and escorted us through the winding paths of the community. The Operation Blessing film crew was following us to document the beginning of this project. The brief ten-minute walk through the streets, with hundreds of eyes watching us, was an eerie feeling—even in broad daylight. We had to complete our work in the daylight hours because it was not a safe place to work at night. The barrios were dangerous places with desperate people living in poverty and squalor.

The site where the community wanted the well was in a small clearing eight feet wide and twelve feet long. It really wasn't enough space to do the work. Randy wasn't discouraged, though, so we began setting up the drill rig and digging the mud pits. Randy enlisted two of the local young men to help with the process. One of the mission agencies that was to receive another Lifewater project sent a workman to assist us, so he could gain experience. So we had six guys. I was really very unimportant at this stage, so I just stood back with a clipboard and answered questions from the local people.

As we began showing our new helpers how to dig the mud pits, it became abundantly clear we had a problem. The overburdened soils were highly contaminated from the years of surface discharge, human waste and garbage. The dirt was black and smelly.

I queried Randy, "We don't have a plug-nickel chance of drilling a good well here, do we?"

Hopeful, he replied, "Let's make the effort anyway."

Everything we knew about identifying a place to drill a well, especially the distance needed to avoid contamination from the local latrines, was compromised. But with Randy's faith we proceeded.

One young mother from the village told me through a translator, "The babies often die because of bad water. We are pleased and thankful you have come to help us with this problem."

The rig was set up with everything ready to go. It was Good Friday. A crowd of people pressed in to watch, and many observed from second-floor windows. They were very curious about what was to take place. There must have been thirty or forty people crowded into the small space, eagerly awaiting an explanation of what was going on. A few were community leaders and understood we were about to drill a well. The others observed the machinery but were unsure what was going to happen.

Crowds often gathered at the start of any Lifewater village water well program. These predictable gatherings offered opportunities to share the gospel while explaining the risky, dangerous and uncertain prospect of constructing a well.

A local man, a policeman who'd become a preacher, asked if he could translate the message I was about to give before we started the drilling process. I stepped up on the dirt pile beside the mud pits we had dug, and he stood beside me.

I began by explaining that we were Christians from the United States who were well drillers. Hearing of the need, we'd been invited by Operation Blessing to visit and see if we could drill successful safe water wells. I then gave a quick warning about the dangers of this process. Gasoline was being used in both engines and the drill was forcing a metal bit that was cutting the well as it drilled. In the process, something could break and hurt someone. Also, the mud pump hoses could burst and spray muddy water everywhere. This is why it was necessary for us to require that everybody stand a safe distance away from the machines while they were running.

Then I offered an explanation for our Christian actions. "Jesus challenges those of us who have been blessed with safe water to help those less fortunate who are forced to drink from contaminated sources."

The policeman-preacher said to me, "Preach it, brother!"

He understood the message and was eager to interpret to the audience. That inspired me to use the Good Friday event to recount what Jesus has done for all of us. Though I didn't understand the Tagalog language, I could tell that the preacher was saying a lot more than I had spoken! I learned later that he also shared John 3:16. That was fine with me since he knew how to communicate so that the people would get the full message. At the conclusion of the message, I offered a prayer that the Lord would bless the well with safe water and the village with better health.

In the afternoon Randy trained the crew to recognize sights and sounds indicating good or bad things happening in the drilling process. We had reached the ninety-foot depth when all of a sudden the drill began bouncing as it hit some very hard rock. Randy chose to stop, withdraw the drills and install a three-inch steel pipe to the bottom of the open hole. He would then pour cement though the pipe, which would create a seal at the bottom. This would give an effective plug in our drilled well at this ninety-foot level. The next day he would return the drill pipes to the well to drill through the cement plug and on to the next layer. He was praying for an aquifer to be below this hardpan layer.

Because I was scheduled to fly home before Randy could complete the well, I missed all of this final construction phase. I learned later that Randy drilled through the cement plug at the bottom of the three-inch pipe so that he could penetrate the hard material we'd encountered on the first day of drilling. Because it was only a foot thick, they broke through to the next layer of soil within a couple hours. It turned out to be some water-bearing sand. Randy was delighted! This meant that if there were no cracks in this layer of hard rock, the surface soil contamination might have been sealed away from the water-bearing aquifer.

In a few days they completed the well, installed a hand pump and began pumping water. The first few hours were spent pumping out drilling mud until the water cleared up. Then Randy took a water sample to the hospital where they could test for microorganisms. A week or so later we received the report from the hospital that the water was safe to drink. It had a very low level of contamination that was acceptable by world standards.

This was one of those hallelujah moments when we praised the Lord for a successful well where human reason and experience said it was impossible. During my twenty-plus years of directing the Lifewater ministry, there have been many special interventions by God. It seems the Lord can always take our efforts, however clumsy, and turn them into successes where He will be glorified.

The following year Randy took his whole family back to the Philippines where he'd taught the local people to drill village wells. This experience helped the whole family, especially his three boys, see what it was like to be a missionary and to put faith to work for the building of the kingdom. Randy's assistance to the local Christian crew brought credibility to the gospel they were preaching. Only in eternity will it be revealed how many found Jesus as Savior and Lord among those served.

One of the partner agencies was New Tribes Mission. Their crew told Randy stories of their years of service in the islands. The island people were very suspicious of strangers. It was difficult to make friends with them. In some places it took years. When other tribes got word that there were foreign workers helping to provide drinking water wells, they were quick to come over the hill and invite the New Tribes Mission trainers to come to their villages. It seemed every new well brought two more tribes requesting their help. How wonderful!

Pastor John James of Operation Blessing set a goal of building one hundred wells from crews trained by Lifewater. In addition to our work with Operation Blessing, Randy Fain trained two other crews from New Tribes Mission and Wycliffe Bible Translators. They, in turn, trained Filipinos to operate these machines. Operation Blessing provided pumps for every well that was completed. In 1999, the year before John went home to be with the Lord, he came to our annual volunteer conference and reported not only that the hundred-well goal had been met but that the Lord had made it possible for them to provide for over three hundred wells.

Three years after our project in the Philippines, the young mother who'd remarked, "The babies often die because of bad water," was located and interviewed. At that time she said, on camera, "The babies don't die anymore." What a wonderful testimony to the change brought by safe drinking water!

CHAPTER 13
Romania: Pollution Control

Staff from Operation Blessing called Lifewater to invite us to participate in a wonderful opportunity assisting the state of Timişoura, Romania, with their nitrate water problems. This request for assistance had been presented to OB by the Romanian government. Farmers and pig ranchers had polluted the aquifer. Over thirty-five years of control by the communist government, demands were placed upon these farmers to increase their productivity by every means possible. The farmers were required to fertilize more than good practice of land management would allow. The pig farmers weren't required to manage the waste, though. Waste management would have increased the cost of production. The nitrate fertilizers and the pig farm wastes were allowed to soak directly into the ground with the natural percolation of rain.

To compound the problem, the communist government allowed these communities to develop normal cities. They had orderly blocks and streets with uniform-size lots for homes. The homes all had small hand-dug wells on their properties for their household water sources. No municipality water systems were developed because the government decided this would be an unnecessary luxury for the people.

Over a couple of decades, this misuse of the environment caused a serious aquifer contamination problem. The excessive farming waste intrusion reached a critical point where human beings could no longer tolerate the high nitrate levels in their water. This was especially true in the health of babies. The most common symptom was a bluish appearance of the skin and serious repercussions from damaged vital internal organs.

Operation Blessing also wanted to help with the orphan problem. This was an additional social problem created by poor human resource management in the communist system. Because the success of the system required "more workers," mothers were encouraged to have as many children as possible. These children were often abandoned and these unwanted children became a burden to society.

Nicolae Ceauşescu, a cruel dictator, was overthrown several months before we arrived. The new Romanian government was willing to allow Operation

Blessing to come in and help with the overcrowded orphanages. They also asked OB if they might help with the widespread water contamination problem. Being a loving Christian agency, Operation Blessing agreed. They promised to obtain competent U.S. engineers to identify, plan and implement remedies to provide communities with safe drinking water. I thank the Lord that they called Lifewater to join them.

By this time Lifewater had grown to include many professional hydrogeologists, water system designers, water chemists and well drillers. We could call on these Christian volunteers to suggest solutions to the problems facing Romania. When OB contacted Lifewater, my first reaction was to call upon Tim Cleath, a hydrogeologist who'd been one of our first volunteers. Tim was pleased with the opportunity and together we planned our strategy. It would be expensive to develop deep community water wells. The project required new modern wells and distribution systems for the twenty-seven cities the Romanian government had selected. Each of these areas contained up to twenty-five thousand people. We worked up an "order of magnitude" budget with a five-year time frame and presented it to Operation Blessing. It was more than $200,000 for equipment and about that much more for labor expenses and additional pieces for the first phase of construction. It was a pay-as-you-go plan, with each phase being funded by the new government if the previous phrase proved successful. The program would then complete additional wells and systems. We were delighted to be invited to present this program to the governor of Timişoura.

Tim and I traveled to Chicago, where we would fly on the Romanian government airline into the capital city of Bucharest. The plane was fully booked. Just before midnight we all boarded a very used 707. (Thank the Lord it was one of the most dependable airplanes Boeing ever built.) As we entered the aircraft and walked through what had once been the first-class cabin section, the seats were missing. Instead, there were boxes and boxes of Timken roller bearings stacked three or four high. Those boxes probably weighed fifty pounds each. They were tethered down with flimsy netting designed to hold lightweight packages. Tim and I exchanged glances as we passed, knowing how dangerous this load could be in turbulent weather, to say nothing of a rough landing. We hoped and prayed the boxes of ball bearings would not be flying through the passenger cabin since we were only ten feet behind them.

The seats in this airliner, soiled and torn, had not been reupholstered in over twenty years. But this was the only way to get where we were going since other airlines had not yet completed contracts with the newly formed Romanian government. The pilots gave the jet full throttle, and we lumbered down the runway loaded to the max or beyond. I thought we would never get airborne. The pilots climbed the jet out at a very slow angle, which was further verification of my suspicions that we were heavily loaded. Thank the Lord for a safe flight.

After a short one-day stay in a very nice, clean hotel and some short meetings with government chaperones, we were ready to work. The government chaperones would act as our interpreters. Immediately following our meetings, Frank, who was the Operation Blessing leader, Tim and I boarded the train for Timişoura. The accommodations were excellent. The ride was first class, smooth and still very inexpensive. The hotels and trains had been kept up well because they'd been used by communist officials.

As we traveled through the night, I could only sleep on and off. I was both excited and still a little woozy from jet travel. The beautiful nighttime countryside was being gently dusted by falling snow. Though the night the Lord was reassuring me that this was the proper thing to do and that He would be guiding us all the way by his footprints unseen.

On our arrival in Timişoura, Pastor Eugène Neigiu, who would become our Christian escort and interpreter, greeted us. He spoke English well. Eugène had been teaching at the university, and he had also pastored an underground Christian church during the communist rule. He took us on a local tour to open our eyes to the tragic history that had changed so abruptly eleven months earlier when the revolution leadership captured President Ceauşescu and his wife.

The next evening, he took us to the newly formed Christian church where he was pastoring. It was a large metal building, 60 by 150 feet, with a single small stage in the front. The rest of the auditorium was packed with chairs filled with people, leaving standing room only. Not only were the chairs all full of people but there were even people looking in the window from outside! The service had been in session for over an hour when we arrived.

Pastor Eugène introduced Tim, who gave a short testimony and sang a solo. Tim has a beautiful singing voice and was received with joyous applause. Thank the Lord our volunteers were prepared to give an answer for the hope that was within them (1 Peter 3:15). Tim did a masterful job as Eugène interpreted his words to the wide-eyed audience, who broke into spontaneous applause at the end. Tim had also explained about a "new hope" Lifewater would bring. They could receive the hope available in Christ and also the hope for clean water in their community. Tim shared how we would be presenting these new plans to the government. When Eugène introduced me, I assured the group that we represented American Christians who were ordinary people just like them. Tim and I were the visual representation of hundreds of believers willing to help. I explained how we all love the same Lord and choose to honor Him by joining Romanian Christians to help their people.

We spent the next day with other Christian leaders and the Operation Blessing local representatives. Together we strategized how to present our relief and development projects to the governor. We also visited a few of the orphanages that day. Words cannot do justice to the tragic conditions we observed in these institutions. The adult workers were doing the best they could with very limited food and supplies and practically no medicine. The rooms and hallways reeked of urine since the meager supply of bleach could not accommodate a thorough cleanup. The babies in dilapidated cribs were a pathetic sight as they reached out for us to pick them up. What was worse was that some of these babies, who'd already given up hope, did not reach out. They just stood in their cribs staring at the wall and swaying back and forth. Tim and I could see why Operation Blessing had such a deep desire to try to rescue these children.

Operation Blessing had a marvelous opportunity to bring important basic needs to the management of these institutions. They would also be able to provide Christian homes for some of the children who were eligible for adoption. In those early days after the revolution it was relatively easy to adopt a child from these orphanages because the government was not yet sufficiently organized to oversee an orderly process of adoption. We all hoped and prayed that those who adopted children would give them loving homes in which they could flourish.

The following day we were to meet with the governor to present our water development project that would begin with the provision of community water wells. Eugène would act as our interpreter, and the four of us—Eugène, Frank, Tim and I—proceeded to his office at the appointed interview time. A handsomely dressed young lady introduced herself as his secretary and asked us to be seated. Then she announced our arrival to the governor.

I was seated next to the desk in her office while the others were waiting in the next room. The door was open so I could see them if they were called in by the governor. During these few moments she expressed some of the terrible conditions her family was experiencing as a result of years of neglect and oppression by Ceauşescu. Her sharing led to a subtle request for me to arrange an opportunity for one of her college-age children to come to America. I told her I was an ordinary citizen and did not have any connections to leverage this kind of immigration privilege. The conversation continued, and I was struck by her desire to see the bells of freedom ring in Romania. She was prepared to do everything in her power to see the new government succeed. And her position afforded her a lot of power that could influence the governor.

The intercom buzzer rang at her desk, and the governor invited her to bring us into his office. As we stood, I reached into my travel bag and retrieved a small bottle of perfume I had brought to share as a special gift when appropriate. I handed her this bottle, and she expressed deep gratitude for the luxury she had apparently never enjoyed.

As we entered the governor's office, he greeted us warmly as we gathered around a large conference table for our discussion. The governor was a large man with a domineering appearance. He had his special interpreter present even though we discovered later that he understood English fairly well. Eugène interpreted for us. We were served another cup of tea and introduced ourselves. We opened our presentation papers, prepared to show our designs for the community development project intended to clean up the contaminated water in the villages of his county jurisdiction.

The plan was a detailed overview of a five-year program that would develop through three phases of work and budget plans. Questions and answers went back and forth for a half an hour. We explained how the first phase was to bring in two medium weight well-drilling machines. They would serve as prototypes for community water-drilling machines. We showed our plan to train Romanians to become well drillers who would eventually be able to produce complete public water distribution systems.

It was a plan that would be replicated in all of the twenty-seven communities in the county. During this introductory phase of the project, Lifewater would train these Romanian crews to operate and maintain the drilling machines. They would also learn about electric submersibles and the distribution systems of pipes, tanks and valves. The second phase would bring in some electrical submersible pumps sized to fit these first representative wells as well as the installation equipment and tools for the pump crews. Lifewater engineers would train local teams during this phase. The final phase would continue our relationship of crew training and consultation as needed. The budget for the project would only be partially subsidized by Operation Blessing and Lifewater, and the balance would need to come from the people of each community.

At the conclusion of this third phase, the work would be totally turned over to a Lifewater-Romania team and become a local for-profit enterprise licensed by the government. It would need to be totally independent, supported by contract work. In addition to the training of the water development team, Lifewater would provide some of the business concepts for planning and managing the systems.

We told the governor we expected to try and raise funds from American churches and individuals for our share of the subsidy. Since it was a very new concept, we could make no promises for how much might be contributed through these sources. We pointed out how well drilling is a very repair-intensive business. One of the most frequently made mistakes by well-drilling contractors is failing to set aside some of the income from well drilling for the odd times when expensive repairs would be needed to carry on the business uninterrupted. Many well drillers missed this strategy and used their profits to buy new trucks or even less important luxuries, so that when the need arose there were insufficient reserves for an unexpected expense. In the worst cases, this ended up in bankruptcy.

The governor seemed delighted by our presentation and somewhat puzzled by our willingness to come to this war-torn country halfway around the world to participate in a program so desperately needed, especially since the people couldn't afford to pay the full cost by themselves. This moment gave us the opportunity to speak an appropriate Christian witness about how Christians count it a privilege to join with other believers in meeting basic human needs. Even more puzzling to him was that it was a program without strings attached. I said Jesus taught us a principle with the story of the Good Samaritan. He is our example of loving Christian behavior when an opportunity arises to care for others. The governor had said he was not a Christian but respected our beliefs and would guarantee our freedom to operate in the country with his approval and assistance. He was known by the revolutionary leadership to be a governor who tried to help the people. Because he was more Romanian than communist, he always landed on the side of helping the people as much as possible. At the end of our meeting he offered a warehouse for the equipment and lodging for Lifewater trainers. Unfortunately his generous offers of anything that cost money never materialized. Because we weren't counting on those perks, the losses didn't inhibit the progress of the Romania Lifewater project.

A government driver and automobile were assigned to shuttle us to a few of the communities that had been suggested for the pilot project. It was interesting to find that most of the mayors in these towns were young men from the revolution. They had been selected by the people for their intelligence, bravery and trustworthiness to be the new leaders. All of them received us warmly.

We also visited a few communities where we took pictures of local people demonstrating the use of backyard hand-operated water wells. Most of them informed us that, for years, people had learned these water wells were so highly contaminated with nitrate that it was causing a sickness. So they showed us how they recovered rainwater for drinking. This source was often inadequate, and many resorted to using a backyard well as their only source of water. They were so pleased to learn of our plan to bring community water wells. These wells would be constructed at sites where tanks and piping systems could supply community water with valve taps at intervals of two hundred meters. This would bring safe water within a convenient proximity of everyone's home.

When we returned to the United States, we made a detailed budget for Operation Blessing to fund as quickly as possible. To our delight they responded by saying, "Go to it, gentlemen. The quicker the better." Lifewater contracted Deep Rock Manufacturing, an American company making well-drilling machines in Arkansas. We ordered two M10 machines complete with drill pipe, bits and repairs. At Shaw Pump I planned the pumping equipment to be as versatile as possible since the depth of the new wells was unknown. I had to accommodate whatever the need would be with broad-range pump performance ability. This flexible equipment would accommodate wells with different levels of aquifers. It would be the challenge of the Lifewater-Romania drilling crew to find aquifers by exploratory drilling that would provide safe drinking water that was sufficiently free from nitrates.

Operation Blessing had a connection with the U.S. government to fly all of our equipment and supplies in a Star Lifter U.S. Air Force transport jet. During our downtime, Pastor Eugène was helping us select a crew to be trained and to develop a profit-making business to be called Lifewater Romania. It was destined to be led by a young, bright, red-headed Christian engineer named Liviu Neagoa. He had ten years of successful leadership, which seemed to be a gift from the Lord. Under his management the company grew to a couple dozen employees and has since stabilized with ten good workers.

In 1999, Randy Fain was the Lifewater volunteer selected to do the training. He was chosen to head up the process of phases 1 and 2. After the equipment arrived, Randy spent several weeks in Romania drilling while training the new Romanian crew as they constructed the first wells. He found that it was impossible for people to use water from the first two aquifers due to nitrate contamination. However, he was able to penetrate the third aquifer, which had a sealed layer of clay. This clay layer sealing it from surface contamination meant that it contained safe water to drink. These deeper aquifers would later be found to be as shallow as two hundred feet and as deep as one thousand feet. The small-sized equipment we had chosen to bring in for phase 1 operations proved to be adequate for a maximum of three hundred feet. Phase 2 would require a much larger air-driven machine. It would be ten times the cost of our small machines.

To the delight of the Romanian crew and the government officials, Randy and crew were producing successful wells that pumped a minimum of 20 gallons per minute and some pumped as many as 120 gallons per minute. Randy also taught the crew about well development and completion along with submersible pump installation, electrical supply management and troubleshooting. Together he and the crew worked in short courses of business management and budget planning.

At his shop in Escondido, California, Randy prepared an air-driven machine to be shipped to Lifewater-Romania for use when he returned the following year. This machine was his own. Driven by his Christian love for these people, he was not only donating it but giving his time and money to ensure it was in excellent working condition. During the following year he prepared for phase 2.

When he returned to the Romania, Randy brought his entire family to spend several months there while he continued the training process. At the next annual Lifewater volunteer conference, he told our volunteers about his family's experience. The children had quickly picked up enough language to be able to play ball with other kids in the street. His family worshipped with the local Romanian Christian church, providing many joyful experiences and friendships during the months of living in Romania.

Randy developed a close Christian relationship with Liviu, the director of Lifewater Romania. But it was also a company-to-company relationship. Randy was supplying the Romania well-drilling crew with operating capital and products to help them get started. During the following years, Randy had to forgive much of the debt because of the costly learning experiences faced while launching the Romanian well-drilling business. This generous Christian man felt the investment was worth it for the kingdom purposes achieved. Through the years he has been proved right over and over again.

In Romania we also worked alongside George and Susan Schmidt, a couple helping an orphanage in Oreadia, Romania. In addition to their water need, the facility was in desperate need of food and supplies. Because the children were spending much time each day carrying water long distances, George and Susan decided a water source on the compound was sorely needed. When they called me I explained what we were doing, and they were ecstatic to know there was a well-drilling company a day's journey away from the Oreadia orphanage. George immediately hired the Lifewater-Romania crew to drill a well at the orphanage. George and Susan raised some money from their church and provided the rest from their own resources.

Knowing the odds against them as they began, Liviu and his crew prayed in front of the many usual onlookers before drilling for a water well. He explained to the crowd, "We can drill a well here, but it will be God who puts water in it."

That first night the crew reported to Liviu that the bit was bouncing very hard at 100 feet. He suggested that the next day they would change to a tri-cone bit. With this modification the crew was able to drill somewhat more smoothly. Progress was slow during the next three or four days. They only saw another 180 feet of depth. The following day of drilling was so difficult that the mud pump couldn't provide adequate circulation and the drilling bit got stuck. To top it off, they were working in very difficult cold and icy conditions. This was tough enough for a normal drilling operation, but now they had to use more hands-on effort retrieving the drill stem and bit. After much prayer, the crew successfully retrieved the drill stem and the bit.

After two more days the crew called Liviu, discouraged. "Three hundred feet, no more drill pipe, and we still have a dry hole. We have no more drill stem. Where do we go from here?"

Liviu brought them another fifty feet of drill stem that he was, by somewhat of a miracle, able to purchase in town. Then he went out there to encourage the crew to press on in the driving cold. Since he felt the Lord had promised him success there, he was determined they should continue. The crew reluctantly agreed to drill some more.

The miracle happened the next day.

They struck an aquifer yielding 127 gallons per minute!

The well at the orphanage was the finest pure water the Romanian crew had experienced. The water rose up in the well to almost become a flowing spring, called an Artesian well. The pump was installed, supplying water to a tank for the entire orphanage. They were even able to supply neighbors. The crew sent us pictures of joyful dancing at the well site as the water sprayed in the air from the pump the crew was using to develop the well.

Susan and George have told this story at the annual Lifewater conference, encouraging many new and old volunteers. It illuminates God's willingness to perform miracles for those willing to step out in faith, following his footprints unseen.

CHAPTER 14
Sudan: Where Women Led the Charge

A request came at a conference in the late 1990s from Voice of the Martyrs to help provide a source of safe water in refugee camps near the Ugandan border in Southern Sudan. I was hesitant to make this opportunity available to volunteers because of the risk factor it presented. There was still military activity between the government forces and the rebels. The Christian rebels were being chased by the Islamic-dominated government and army who opposed any Christian expression in the country. Hearing about the possibility, Cathy, a volunteer team leader, approached me to ask if she might consider leading this project. We had a long private talk.

Cathy Fitzgerald had a Ph.D. in hydrology. She was teaching at a university in Reno, Nevada, and had her own private consulting company. She was well qualified for the task at hand. But because I was concerned about the dangerous area where she would have to work, I explored the risk with her. She was so taken by the request from Voice of the Martyrs, and their appeal for these desperate people, that she set aside her own personal safety in response to her conviction that the Holy Spirit was calling her to do this job with His protection.

She did a masterful job planning and communicating with all the parties involved. Cathy obtained her visa from Uganda to travel to the border area. She planned to enter Sudan with a Voice of the Martyrs representative from an airport near the border. After a flight from the United States in a commercial jet, she arrived in Kampala, Uganda. After a day for jet lag recovery, she took a local flight north to the border. On arrival she joined the local contact and set out on a series of bus and Jeep rides to arrive at the refugee camp just outside the city of Yea.

The director at the camp was aware of her trip plans and had detailed for her the obstacles keeping them from obtaining safe water. Cathy knew ahead of time that there was a small contaminated freshwater stream nearby. She hoped that the conditions would allow her to build an infiltration gallery, providing a natural sand filter and collection basin. The refugees could draw clean water from this point—clean, but not yet safe. She would teach them to use chlorine to purify the water for drinking.

With help from the director of the camp, tools, cement and lumber for Cathy's design were gathered and brought to the site. Many young men assisted her in digging the chambers of the facility. One setback, a cave-in of one of the forms, created a delay that put completion of the system before Cathy's scheduled departure at risk. Graciously, the Lord provided. The system was close enough to completion before Cathy left for her to give instructions allowing the refugee camp workers to finish and operate this system.

The night before she returned, the Islamic government army bombed the city of Yea. God reminded Cathy of the dangerous reality she faced but assured her she was still under His protection. Cathy's report during the next Lifewater annual conference elicited many new participants for the next project in the Sudan.

A second opportunity to serve in the Sudan was led by Patricia Hettinger (Klever). The plan was to introduce the LS-100 water well drilling machine to a few trainees at the refugee camp. We shipped a brand-new rig to our partners in Uganda, at World Wide Ministries. They needed a new rig and were willing to donate their used one to this refugee camp. Pat was a seasoned surface water hydrologist and volunteer who I could trust going into a very risky environment. The area was one where the government soldiers had chased refugees into small camps along the border with Kenya. Sonia Granada, our secretary at Lifewater, announced to me that she would like to go as Pat's assistant. This was not an easy decision for me. She was confident the Holy Spirit wanted her to go, but I was not so sure that this was a wise first trip for her. I asked her to confirm this calling with her church pastor and family to obtain their support and approval. She did so and raised the money for her expenses from her church and family.

Pat and Sonia arrived in Kampala, Uganda, and met up with the Uganda Lifewater drilling team. They inspected the drilling machine that was to be used to train the Sudanese drilling crews. It had some wear but was in operative condition. It would certainly drill the few wells they needed in the camps and would provide an excellent tool for training a new crew to provide village water wells in the area. The Ugandan crew drove the truck and rig on a fourteen-hour journey to the Sudan border while Pat and Sonia flew by local commercial air service to a small airport near the border.

When Pat and Sonia arrived and got off the airplane, they found themselves in a lonely place with a small shack as the airport facility. No one was there to greet them. Not long after they arrived, a gentleman with a Jeep, who was heading to the refugee camp, offered to drive them. Without his help, they would have been stranded. I was glad this happened without my knowledge, because I would have had a heart attack had I known the dangers they were facing!

Wearing her hard hat and fatigues, Patricia set up the rig at the well site and showed the local volunteers how to dig the mud pits to begin the process of drilling a well.

CHAPTER 15
Tanzania: The Most Likely of Places to Start

In 1981 and 1983, Lifewater hosted a booth at the Billy Graham conference for pastors and evangelists in Amsterdam. The Billy Graham organization had provided each of these evangelists with small business cards to offer to organizations in the exhibit hall. This was an easy and quick way to connect with the agencies. During their free time between sessions, these evangelists would walk through the exhibit hall and talk with the agencies represented. Lifewater was one of about fifteen exhibiting Christian ministries to support these evangelists with projects to connect the "word and deed" outreach.

Hundreds of pastors stopped by my Lifewater booth to discuss water problems in their areas. They'd stop as I began a talk at the booth, about every ten minutes, about providing safe drinking water to the poor. At the beginning of my speech, five or six pastors strolling by our booth would stop to listen when they heard the word "water." By the time I'd concluded my speech, about four minutes later, there were usually fifteen to twenty listening intently. It didn't take them long to be gushing about the ways they would be able to partner with Lifewater. From among more than ten thousand evangelists who attended the two Amsterdam Billy Graham gatherings, Lifewater chose thirty-seven as those serving in the most likely places in the world to begin projects.

Pastor Richard ("Dick") Mulimuka was one of those. He directed the development division of the Tanzania Moravian Church, and he was hopeful we could launch a project there. Dick wrote a fine letter to me as soon as he returned to Tanzania. As our staff sorted through the two thousand requests from over one hundred countries, his agency and outreach ministry seemed a very likely candidate for the Lifewater village water well strategy. After corresponding with him, it was clear to me this fit our ministry to a T. We even decided to attempt this project without the expense of a survey trip.

I chose to circumvent our normal plan of implementation in order to conserve time and dollars. In an attempt to take as much risk out of "jumping into a drill training program on the first trip," I had several phone conversations with Dick that convinced me of his ability to gather the leadership of his church for a conference. This is where we would demonstrate the small well-drilling machine. We would show how developing village water wells in areas where people were drinking from open sources containing waterborne diseases could be useful. This ministry of the Tanzanian Moravian Church would greatly improve their gospel outreach program.

Back at our office in South El Monte, California, we prepared a complete drilling rig, packing supplies and extra parts in the shipping crate. We sent it off by freighter ship. The freighter developed engine trouble and had to offload all the cargo to another ship. This delayed the arrival of our drilling machine by one month. I was hoping to be able to take our team to Tanzania sooner, but this delay meant we'd miss the best window of opportunity, during summer months. We changed our plans to accommodate the delay when we finally received notice that the ship had arrived in port. We also notified Dick Mulimuka so he could retrieve the shipment.

After two months of trying to find our shipment, the Port Authority communicated to us that the container with our drilling rig had been stolen. We waited another month, but it was never found. Was this still something the Lord wanted us to do? There were so many obstacles and delays, I was beginning to wonder if it was the Lord saying, "Don't do this now." Or was it just the handiwork of the Devil throwing roadblocks in the way of this project he opposed? The Lord spoke to my conscience, urging me to persevere.

Then we made a big decision. We decided to reboot and take a rig with us on an airplane! A Lifewater volunteer named Amos Broughton and I packed up a drilling rig in nineteen boxes. They contained extra supplies, training literature and even some canned food items we would consume while we were there. We wouldn't disappoint the Tanzanian leadership who'd waited so patiently for us to put on a conference at Tabora, in central Tanzania. I decided Amos, Lorraine and I would carry it all with us from Los Angeles to Dar es Salaam, the capital. We paid the extra duty for all the additional pieces we were shipping and boarded a British Airways flight.

Official after official wanted to know what we were doing with all of the equipment and how it was going to be used. They were concerned we would sell the equipment and wanted to collect an import duty before they would release it to us.

Lorraine and I boarded a British Airways flight in London that stopped in Cairo, Egypt, and Khartoum, Sudan. In Cairo there was a bomb threat when it was discovered that someone had written on a lavatory mirror, "There is a bomb on this airplane." The British Airways crew took the threat very seriously and radioed ahead. The police and bomb-sniffing dogs inspected the entire aircraft before anyone was allowed to disembark. Once in the terminal, we all had to wait to be searched. It took several hours. Everyone's luggage, and the nineteen boxes of drilling rig, were laid out on the tarmac next to the plane. Each passenger had to identify each piece that belonged to them for it to be returned to the cargo hold, before we could proceed on to Dar es Salaam. Thank the Lord the threat was an empty one, and we finally arrived at the airport to clear customs early in the afternoon. We were six hours late.

When we finally arrived, we expected the duty charge to be 100 percent of the value. After an hour of pleading, we convinced the Port Master customs agent that we were Christian missionaries and that the equipment was for the benefit of the Tanzania Moravian Church, not a business enterprise to be sold. This caused another hour delay. He finally gave us permission to enter duty free. Praise the Lord!

We had only a few Tanzanian shillings that we'd exchanged in America to tide us over until we got to the Dar es Salaam Hotel. I asked a customs official where I could change dollars into shillings. He pointed to a bank window in the airport where I traded in 100 U.S. dollars for 1,500 Tanzanian shillings. This was a "legal" transaction recorded on our official entry forms that we were required to carry on our persons throughout our visit in Tanzania. On the street, black market shillings were available for forty or fifty to one dollar. Naturally this discrepancy in value made our shillings worth much less. The Tanzanian economy was running on the black market rate.

Lorraine and I were ecstatic when we were finally on our way out of customs. She and I had to push all the boxes and luggage into the holding area in order to load them up on the Moravian Church truck, which was supposed to meet us.

But no one showed up.

What would we do? We had no idea where the Moravian Church headquarters was. We had a street name but no number. Most of the young men with their white Islamic head caps turned away from helping us. We really felt helpless. Finally two young men identified themselves as Christians and helped us find a taxi driver who knew where we were going.

The men carried all of our luggage and boxes out to this taxi. There were boxes hanging out the windows, in the trunk and in the back seat with me. Best of all, these two Christian fellows helped us hire him for a reasonable fee.

At the Tanzania Moravian Church headquarters we received an apology for the mix-up. They thought we were coming in on another flight. They were very helpful getting us settled in the hotel where Lorraine and I crashed. Jet lag, bomb threats, custom hassles, and hot, humid weather took its toll on both of us. We drew water for a bath that looked like the muddy water in a ditch in front of our home in California. The hotel officials blamed it on the rains, which had gotten into the city systems. This is one of the biggest dangers for a municipal water supply. Nevertheless the water felt good. We just closed our eyes to the color. A single lightbulb hanging from a cord lit our room. It glowed bright and dim with the power fluctuations.

Welcome to the developing world.

The next day we met up with Amos and boarded a Mission Aviation Fellowship Cessna for the three-hour flight to Tabora. The drilling rig and all of our equipment was being transported by truck and would arrive three days later, before our conference demonstrations would need to begin. After our MAF pilot refueled in Mwanza, we took off for our final leg to Tabora. The three of us enjoyed the beautiful view of the vast open plains of Tanzania. We also flew over villages with grass huts and animals roaming free in the Kalahari.

It was a wonderful celebration to finally arrive at Pastor Mulimuka's church headquarters. The guest facilities were far better than the hotel we'd left behind in Dar es Salaam. Lorraine and I had a comfortable room with two beds and mosquito nets. The toilet and shower were six doors down the wood-slat path outside. The strange-sounding insects kept us awake until late evening, and a large chorus of croaking frogs woke us up early just before sunrise. Does it sound difficult? The spiritual purposes of Lifewater's beginning made all of these experiences joyful events! All of this was God's purpose. We needed these late evening and early morning times to pray and study the Word for wisdom and strength.

The Ougali meals they served were adequate, but thankfully Lorraine and I had a stash of canned tuna and chicken to augment them. One evening an entire nest of army ants was on the move right by our front door. One of the Tanzanian workmen came over with a can of gas, some matches, and a broom. He created a barrier of fire between the ants and us while he disrupted their march by stamping his feet and sweeping them away in a very interesting dance-like action. It was obvious he had done this before and was able to avoid the stings.

The next day ten to fifteen of the top Moravian Church leaders arrived for our conference. This was a very important event for them. Some had traveled two days to be with us. Lifewater subsidized half of their travel and meals. We opened the conference with a round of introductions and each person shared their expectations for the event. It inspired me to hear how many were willing to work hard to see our program succeed with their church community development programs. As in most projects in the developing world, there were a few who were in it for what they could get out of it. We identified these individuals and tried to help them understand that we were not rich Americans but Christians who had come at our own expense to help them with a very important "word and deed" ministry to their communities.

Lorraine had come prepared to help the ladies learn how to make soap. We'd brought all of the tools and ingredients with the exception of the animal fat and vegetable oil. The Tanzanian ladies group had been prepared to bring these last two items. Instead of animal fat, though, they brought beeswax. The process began by melting the beeswax. One of the local pastors, who was there to observe the process, noticed that a few bees started to buzz around.

He remarked, "Soon there will be very many bees."

We learned something that day: Don't try to make soap with beeswax. Bees can smell it for miles and will come to protect their construction material! Lorraine and the team took the mixture into a sealed room and finished the task. The ladies were delighted to learn this process that would help them make a little money. But more importantly, the soap would provide a valuable contribution to community sanitation. Contaminated hands pass on disease more than any other carrier. The women made a second batch outside, this time with the animal fat and a beautiful wood mold for the soap.

The S100 Stover rig arrived by truck on time. Amos went to work welding up the drill couplings and drill pipe that the local church supplied on site. The five-foot drill pipes were the only things we didn't bring on the airplane with us. Amos had to work with an arc welder who didn't have quite enough power to properly attach the couplings. Drilling caused the crew to experience a failure of one of these joints, terminating our demonstration. Thankfully we were able to drill enough footage so that all the participants were able to observe the whole rotary mud well-drilling process.

The next day Pastor Mulimuka had scheduled us to visit the Ussoka School, a couple of hours away from Tabora. In the morning he, Amos, Lorraine and I rode in the Jeep on a rough dirt road with the usual potholes and loose sand. At noon we stopped on this lonely road to eat our brown bag lunch. We were truly out in the middle of nowhere. A map of Tanzania shows Tabora in the middle of the country. Hundreds of miles in any direction had populations of small villages separated by many miles. Our lunch spot on the road was a beautiful open high plains area with unusual flowers and savanna brush. The air was clear, and the silence was conducive to recognizing the Holy Spirit reassuring us of God's leading.

We arrived at the school after lunch and were greeted by a missionary couple from Canada. They were teachers of mathematics and biology at the Ussoka School. The most urgent problem they were facing now was a lack of water in their relatively modern piped water system. The source of water was a lake one thousand meters to the south where a pump house used to provide the entire school with water. They wanted us to see and diagnose the problem.

We set out on foot to the lake, walking through tall elephant grass, oblivious to the cobras slithering in the grass. When we arrived at the pump house, the schoolmaster opened the door to the room where the pump should have been. He explained to us that the government had confiscated the pump to be used at one of their high-priority locations. The school was left to fend for themselves in finding a new pump. They had been doing without one for over a year. There were no prospects to get the school fully operating again by replacing it. Lorraine and I were heartbroken over this.

The next day we were invited to journey to the Leper Hospital at Sekonga, about a five-hour journey over the same type of dirt roads. This time, because of the distance, we would stay overnight. The kitchen staff at the school had prepared us a nice lunch of sandwiches and fruit to enjoy halfway through the trip.

When we arrived at the hospital, we met two Dutch missionary couples who were directing the efforts there. More than a dozen patients in the hospital had leprosy, most in very advanced stages. Their hands and feet were badly distorted or even missing. Dr. Johansson explained their water problem: The source was an open pond filled with all kinds of contaminants that most Americans wouldn't put a foot in to rinse it off after a hot march! Lorraine and I could not believe our eyes. He also shared his other needs for medicines and equipment.

As we walked into the courtyard, we saw five patients sitting on the ground playing an African game. It consisted of two rows of six depression cups made in the ground. It begins with four stones in each of the cups. Each player takes a turn to scoop up one handful of stones from a cup and proceeds to place one stone from his hand in the sequence of twelve consecutive cups. At the end of dropping stones in the cups, if the player adds one stone in the last cup to make a total of four, he then removes the stones as his prize and proceeds to have another turn of scooping and placing stones. The winner is the player who gathers the most number of stones. I was fascinated with the game and later purchased a wooden model, called Mancala, at a gift shop near the airport before we journeyed home. I had a lot of fun teaching my granddaughters and grandsons this game.

The hospital had a guesthouse for Lorraine and me. Helpers carried several five-gallon buckets of water for us to be able to bathe. They were very generous to care for us tender Americans. We had mosquito nets for protection, but Lorraine didn't trust them. She got out her can of Raid and sprayed the rooms windows and corners. I don't know which was worse, breathing those fumes or risking a mosquito bite! We both chose protection over the odor. We were warned not to go outside at night to use a bathroom since there were cobras in the grass.

After one more day at Tabora, the Tanzanian leaders wanted us to visit one more place in desperate need of safe water. It was a refugee camp, 150 kilometers north of town. The fifty-acre camp had become home to refugees who'd fled the wars in Burundi and the Congo. They'd been allowed by the Tanzanian government to make temporary homes on this land, but no other assistance was offered. We arrived at the camp, named Kigwa, to find a director awaiting our arrival. He showed us several hand-dug wells where the water level was standing about eight feet down. The water table in this area was about eight to ten feet underground.

Lorraine and I filmed many scenes of people accessing contaminated water from these open sources and this hand-dug well. We had high hopes that these desperate scenes would create a compelling video that would elicit compassion on the part of our donors to help these desperate refugees obtain assistance from Lifewater. We hoped that by showing these folks how to clean up the wells and install hand pumps it would provide a continuous source of safe drinking water.

On the way back we stopped along the roadside after a gentle rain because I wanted to videotape some of the beautiful countryside we were passing. I suggested that I would like to film a scene of the Jeep coming toward me down the road. I had our driver back the Jeep up some five hundred meters and proceed toward me, waving as they passed on down the road. Of course they were supposed to stop when I waved that the videotaping was over. As a joke the team decided to continue driving and leave me stranded in the middle of nowhere. I wondered if Lorraine had paid them off to help her be rid of the crazy guy with the video camera. When they'd had their fun, they returned for me.

The next day we began our journey home by loading into a twin Otter Tanzania Airliner for our flight back to Dar es Salaam.

CHAPTER 16
Uganda: The Ravages of War

A U.S. team was invited to help the government of Uganda relocate thousands of refugee families who had fled to the cities to escape the country's civil war. The area chosen for this project was the Kaokamoli area in central Uganda. This was a lush, rich virgin farmland much like the Central Valley of California would have been in the 1800s.

The Karamojong herdsmen inhabited the area very sparsely, traveling with their cattle during changing seasons. There was plenty of vacant land the government could use to redistribute to refugee families who could become subsistence farmers with government assistance. The government was counting on Christian agencies such as Lifewater to assist in this major project. The team of experts invited by the Uganda government included one agronomist, one medical doctor, one Christian school principal, one contractor, two Kenyan interpreters who spoke five Kenya languages and myself, for the water resource development issues.

We arrived in Nairobi and spent the day recovering from jet lag. We spent the next full day in a meeting planning our strategy and our trip to the Kaokamoli government conference. Ernie and Marilyn, the local missionaries ministering to orphaned children in this area, were hosting this meeting at the orphanage compound. This compound had been Idi Amin's prison farm, with four well-built concrete buildings that were being used by Marilyn for the orphanage housing.

We flew on an Aero Commander, landing on a dirt runway that had been prepared by the missionaries. Then we drove the forty-five-minute ride to the facility in two Jeeps, arriving just before sunset. It was still dangerous to be out at night. Bands of thugs, with guns and knives, robbed and stole anything of value wherever and whenever they could. We learned the morning after we arrived that a young man had just been killed for his machete.

Marilyn fed us a wonderful stew that first night. In the evening we shared a time of prayer and fellowship. The government was planning to offer thousands of acres that had been divided into five-acre parcels in the hopes of alleviating the catastrophic problem facing overcrowded cities. Scarcity of food, increase in crime, improper sanitation, compromised water supplies and inadequate housing were some of the problems they hoped to rectify with this relocation plan.

We had cots and mosquito nets to keep us as comfortable as possible for the week of work ahead of us. The U.S. team was prepared for the change of pace, environment and living conditions. It was a small matter to put up with these inconveniences since we were confident the Lord had called us to the assignment.

Uganda officials who'd invited us to participate in the conference began arriving throughout the next day. There were two members from parliament, several high-ranking military personnel and the team of fifteen Ugandan Marines who'd been assigned to protect us all. We took a couple of trips out into the areas being proposed by the government as the prototypes of the land parcels to be distributed to refugee families. On one trip I spotted a canyon with a watershed that could be captured by an earthen dam. Because I'd brought topographical maps, I was able to locate this area and determine the approximate amount of water it would hold. With average rainfalls the dam could hold and distribute enough water to irrigate several square miles of this beautiful farmland.

I had only read in books about the construction of such a dam and the approximate costs. My presentation to the group was a very rough estimate of time and dollars. I tried to be conservative so that my estimations were not a disappointment to the government personnel. They needed to have a clear understanding of the enormous costs that this water development project would require.

I asked the Marines if we could hike off the road to survey this canyon to identify the approximate location where the dam could be constructed. They exchanged glances and suggested that it was dangerous to hike up through the six-foot-tall elephant grass to the spot about a mile away.

I convinced them that I needed to see the site to help me determine the feasibility. Reluctantly they agreed and we started the march up the valley. Two Marines with automatic weapons led the way while the rest of us made lots of noise so as not to surprise any wild animals. We could hear the chatter of animals recognizing our presence. We saw some baboons and heard the noise of larger animals in the distance. It was quite a noisy chorus. It wasn't long before we came upon a site where the elephant grass was all smashed down in a circle about eight feet in diameter.

One of the Marines looked at me, pointed to the ground and said, "Something very big was just lying there moments ago." I suddenly realized what they meant about danger! Being that close to large animals in the wild was not something I'd ever experienced.

We finally arrived at the spot that appeared to me to be about 200 feet above the valley where the canyon narrowed, with two steep sides about 150 feet apart. I climbed up one side and took some pictures for reference. This narrow canyon passage seemed ideal since there was evidence of rapid moving water scouring the sides and bottom to bedrock. I didn't try to estimate how high the dam would need to be to hold back a reservoir adequate for the relocation project. This would take a team of surveyors and engineers with better skills than mine. But the survey I conducted became an important consideration for the plan, so I'm glad we did it! Thankfully we all returned to the Jeeps safely.

At our final day of planning, each of the experts prepared a paper to present to the Ugandan government that detailed our final assessment of the project. Developing safe water for the community would be less costly using boreholes and pumps in the valley. They could be positioned along the roadside at convenient intervals. To provide abundant irrigation water year-round from an earthen dam was a much larger expense. Since this dam seemed too ambitious for the beginning of the settlement, I suggested that we could provide small drilling machines for accessing safe drinking water in the developing communities at reasonable distances from each home. This seemed to be the more likely scenario that they would adopt should the other entire plan prove too costly.

The contractor and one of the government military generals suggested that security would be the most difficult problem to overcome. They said that selecting these families in the cities, where they were just squatters, would have long-range ramifications for their immediate family and friends. It was suggested that a green card could be passed out to the head of a family that would give the family five hectares each. The drawback to this plan, though, was that relatives who did not receive a green card would insist on settling with the uncle who did. So instead of one family, there might end up being five or six families on each plot of land. One absurd solution was presented: construct machine gun towers to protect the people who have the right to settle this land. Most of us pointed out that this wasn't practical and would be counterproductive to helping people live in peace.

The contractor presented a wonderful plan describing how the roads and streets would be developed. The agronomist presented a strategy to phase in common crops grown by farmers in Uganda, trees and other cash crops, teaching the refugees who may not have farming experience. Thankfully, the physician cited the need for health and sanitation training and facilities to keep diseases suppressed in this remote region where medical attention would be scarce to nonexistent. He also pointed out how important safe drinking water would be to this developing community.

We had a wonderful meal together and celebrated our unity of diverse cultures that had come together to plan a community to help the poorest of the poor. After our celebration meal our packed bags were loaded into the Jeep for our return trip home. The missionary radioed ahead to the pilot and explained that we would arrive at the runway at exactly 1:00 p.m. This careful coordination was necessary to avoid the mass of people who, when they heard the sound of the Jeep heading toward the runway, would come to see the airplane and the people boarding it.

The ride was forty-five minutes, so at 12:15 we climbed into the Jeep and drove off toward the airstrip. When we were fifteen minutes from the runway, people began coming out of the grasslands and running down the road behind the Jeep. As misfortune would have it, the airplane was nowhere in sight. The major worry was that some of the gangs of hoodlums with guns would also make their way to the airstrip. We waited in the Jeep for about fifteen minutes. By that time there were about twenty adults and forty children all surveying us as the strange exotic creatures we were. Soon six guys with guns strolled up very casually with their weapons slung over their shoulders. They told our Kenyan interpreters that they were the local militia. Right!

The doctor and I were sitting in the back seat having a casual conversation. Two of the young men spoke broken English. One leaned into the back of the Jeep and asked who we were and what we were doing there. The doctor told them briefly about our project of refugee resettlement. One leaned over and asked me what I was doing with this group. I told them I was the water engineer. He immediately asked me if I would come with him down the road a little to see a broken hand pump and what could be done about it.

I had just taken a few pictures of them, and I casually climbed out of the Jeep, took the camera strap off my neck and handed it to the doctor. I then proceeded to walk with these fellows down the road. Two got in front of me, two alongside, and two behind. I immediately felt very uncomfortable with this formation. I was no more than a hundred feet away from the Jeep when the guy on my right side asked me for my baseball cap.

This was a red flag that I'd been warned about. We'd been instructed not to give them anything because it could start a riot. Everybody would want to have something.

So I simply mumbled something about, "Well, maybe back at the Jeep."

The fellow on my left, seeing my passport sticking out of my shirt pocket, asked me if he could see my passport. A second big red flag: passports were worth $1,000!

I put my right hand over my passport and muttered, "Maybe I better go back and wait for the airplane."

I immediately turned around and began walking back to the Jeep. The two guys behind me parted and allowed me to walk back past them.

One of the ones who spoke the best English protested, "Oh no! We are friends."

I just kept walking.

It was a beautiful day with birds and butterflies and greenery all around. At that moment I had a very strong sense of my friends back home praying for me.

As I walked back and sat down in the Jeep, the doctor asked me, "What happened?"

I just said, "Later."

Suddenly I was glad for the several dozen adults and children crowded around our Jeep! The environment was full of beauty and peace as the six young men slowly gathered around again. I'm sure the press of the crowd insulated us from any harm these guys would like to have imposed on us had we been alone. As they returned they weren't asking any more questions. This time there were no happy faces.

Thankfully the airplane arrived just a few minutes later. As the pilot offloaded supplies for the orphanage, we loaded our bags and climbed aboard. The pilot let me take the copilot seat since I knew how to fly. It had been a long time since I'd been behind the stick, but I was looking forward to taking the yoke. As we began to ascend, I related the event of my aborted walk with the six "militia men." Everybody had wondered why I had returned so quickly, and now they knew!

I didn't start breathing easy until we were twelve thousand feet over the Rift Valley.

One month later I received the bad news that these young men with guns, or others just like them, had surrounded the Aero Commander and confiscated the fifty-five-gallon drum of fuel that had been brought for the orphanage vehicle. They also seized the airplane, demanding some sort of bribe. Some weeks later I also heard that two of the nurses from another mission in the area were killed. It was a very dangerous spot. There were no good answers for these tragedies this side of eternity.

These, and other incidents like them, were major obstacles for the government to overcome while implementing the refugee relocation project we had just sketched out. Yet the local team pressed on, helping those who were poor in spite of these dangers.

Christians have been called to share the good news for hundreds of years, facing dangers while trusting in Jesus' promise: "I am with you always, to the very end of the age" (Matthew 28:30). This local team carried on their ministry of helping the poor in spite of danger.

CHAPTER 17
Uzbekistan: The Poisonous Aral Sea

Odo had been a blessing to Lifewater ever since he'd come to us from Mission Aviation Fellowship. One of Odo's first big assignments was to travel to the Aral Sea in Uzbekistan. Our Lifewater volunteer Tim Cleath, a hydrogeologist, and Dr. Frost, of San Diego State University, joined him on this assignment. In Tashkent they attended a conference for experts working on the problem of contaminated public water facilities resulting from fertilizers and insecticides that had leached into canals and the groundwater. These contaminants were also present in high concentrations in the irrigation ditches from which people were drawing drinking water. Expectant mothers were giving birth to children with serious physiological birth defects. Some were so severe that the number-one cause of death of young women was immolation. These women would set themselves on fire in protest of the damage being done to the health of the people by the government from their failure to provide safe water supplies.

The following year, Odo and Tim had shipped our small drilling rig to a site where the Uzbek government water department facilities and personnel were stationed. Odo demonstrated the machine to these Uzbek well drillers. They were unimpressed since, in their opinion, their diesel-truck-mounted core-drilling machines were much faster. So Odo and the Uzbek team had a race! Each drilled a well and completed it in a single day. The Uzbek team drilled the well quicker, but it took them the rest of the day to complete it. Odo's well came in second. But its construction provided access to the aquifer below without contamination from the surface, like the fast Uzbek well drillers' machine was causing. Odo showed them how to properly protect their wells for future construction.

Over the years Odo went back to these Uzbek friends several times, contracting with them to construct wells. Hiring them ensured that the community had access to safe water supplies as quickly and affordably as possible. The Uzbek team was constructing wells for us at the ridiculously low price of $25 each because the communists never trained their people with good business management skills. They soon realized this price was too low, so the next hundred wells were priced at $40 each—still way under their costs. By the time they were completing the four-hundredth well, we were paying $125 each. An additional benefit was that these payments were helping the newly formed local well-drilling company to survive. It was also less expensive than if we'd produced these wells and trained new people. It was a great bargain to offer churches and other donors in America who wanted to provide a village well for a community.

The government turned over the whole project to the employees when the Soviet Union collapsed. They were paid the equivalent of twelve dollars per month until they got the business going. This was just enough money for each employee to buy potatoes and bread for his family. A local team of Christian development workers from Youth With a Mission, or YWAM, partnered with us to monitor the construction and water quality of the wells this crew was constructing before we paid them. It was a good relationship since the people were getting good drinking water wells at a decent price.

I remember one story Odo told me about the first wells the Uzbek crews drilled for Lifewater. He'd explained to them that it was necessary to pour a concrete pad around the well to eliminate surface water contamination. The next day he went out with the crew to observe their construction technique. The crew had just taken cement from a wheelbarrow and dumped it in a pyramid-like shape around the well, making it impossible for anyone to stand on what should have been a flat cement floor.

Odo explained to the water development director that this is not what he had in mind for a cement pad. They gathered the crew at this sloppy construction site and explained once again the size and shape that was necessary for good construction techniques. It was hard work smoothing out the concrete into a flat smooth surface. But the next one was properly prepared and Odo approved it for payment.

CHAPTER 18
Zambia: Where Women Bear the Water

One day in 1992 I received a letter from director of the Evangelical Fellowship of Zambia, Joseph Imakando. Joseph had been educated in England, elected president of the Fellowship and pastored a church in the capital city of Lusaka. He had first met me in our booth at the Amsterdam Billy Graham conference for pastors and evangelists.

He introduced me to a couple specifically skilled to fit the needs of a water project in Zambia. The missionary couple were Helmut and Esther Reuter. Helmut was an engineer sent by his church in Germany to Zambia. He and his wife, Esther, a registered nurse, had been called to explore new projects there that would be "word and deed"-type ministries. Esther was ministering to the women's groups with health and hygiene training that would also bring to them the gospel message about the need for a clean soul along with a clean body. Lifewater has a training module for health and hygiene called "Clean Hands, Clean Heart." Esther's program was similar. Helmut and Esther had been commissioned to organize a community development program for the Fellowship.

Helmet and Joseph followed up with Lifewater to explore the possibility of a relationship that would assist their churches with a long-range program to meet the community's need for safe drinking water.

After a few months of aerogram letters and long-distance telephone conversations, we laid out a program to begin the partnership process. This was another one where I took the large economic risk of skipping an important first step: the survey trip. We decided to jump right to the program by shipping the equipment and tools in order to begin immediately. We would start right out demonstrating and training local nationals to operate the well-drilling machine.

Lifewater prepared a shipment of one S100 Stover well-drilling rig and supplies for an air shipment to Lusaka. It had been my standard operating procedure to wait until we had heard that the shipment cleared customs before moving forward. Then when we were informed it was safely on the mission compound at the headquarters, and nothing had been lost, stolen or broken, we'd take the next step. We would not proceed, by purchasing airline tickets or arranging other plans, before these things were done.

I convinced Greg Hamer, a committed Christian man and a hydrogeologist, to agree to travel with Lorraine and me when we visited Zambia. While we were waiting for the rig's arrival we had several meetings to detail the most efficient plan for introducing the village water well program. We decided it would be important for us to hold a conference in Zambia, a three-day working seminar and demonstration event, which Joseph and Helmut would organize. Twenty-two pastors and development committee workers registered for the conference. Joseph also assured Lorraine that there would be a dozen or more nurses and women's group leaders for her portion of the Lifewater training. As a nurse, she was coming to introduce the importance of safe water, health and a hygiene development program. These women were delighted to participate. They knew she was also going to help them learn how to make soap, a contribution to the community's health and hygiene and a possibility for a wage-earning skill using locally available natural resources. All of the equipment and information we were providing would remain the possession of the Evangelical Fellowship of Zambia.

The Zambia team had picked out a site for the conference grounds and accommodations that included an area large enough for us to demonstrate the drilling process. Since some participants would be required to travel a considerable distance, we agreed to subsidize the expense by offering the round-trip bus fare for each person invited to attend. We felt it was going to be a very efficient use of time and money.

Greg, Lorraine and I boarded a British Airways jet bound for Lusaka, Zambia, with stops in London and Kenya. The flight was smooth and uneventful through to Nairobi, Kenya. The excitement came on the Kenyan Airlines flight from Nairobi to Zambia.

The jet was an aging 707. When the pilot started the engines, one backfired unusually loud. He turned them off and mechanics came out to inspect them. After a few minutes they replaced the cowling on the engine and determined it was airworthy. We took off about half an hour late. Just a little before the halfway point between the airports, the pilot announced we had to turn back to repair defective altimeters. We arrived back at the

Nairobi Airport so mechanics could exchange the altimeters. Now we were two and a half hours late. It was necessary to refuel in Malawi's Lilongwe airport. After a short exchange of passengers, on and off, the pilot started the engines again for our last leg to Lusaka, Zambia.

This time one of the two compressors experienced bearing failure. The screeching noise was deafening. The pilot didn't notice, though, until smoke began to fill the cabin. He immediately switched it off and the crew opened the doors to let out the smoke.

Greg was sitting about five rows ahead of Lorraine and me. He turned to look at me when he saw the smoke. We exchanged a glance, agreeing silently, "Smoke inside of airplanes is not good." The Lord kept us in our seats, though we were both quite apprehensive.

In a few minutes the smoke cleared and the pilot elected to fly on to our final destination. By now our delay meant we'd arrived in Lusaka at nighttime, when we should have arrived in the afternoon. Joseph was there to meet us after we cleared customs and we all proceeded to the curbside pickup. Then we enjoyed a twenty-four-hour recovery day at the guest house provided by Helmut and Esther Reuter.

Before we had bought our tickets we had been assured that the shipment had arrived. I was told there wouldn't be any problem getting through customs and that they were waiting for a truck to pick it up and bring it to the compound. However, when we arrived the rig was still not at the compound. Fortunately, Joseph was a good negotiator and had friends at the custom dock. The day after our arrival they picked up the shipment. Praise the Lord there were no import fees.

The next day Greg and I, with a few young Zambian men, set up the rig in a yard where we could assemble the components and test them. We wanted to be sure that our demonstration before all these pastors would be successful. It took us a few hours to make the assembly in the garage and bring the drilling rig out to the chosen site for a trial run. Before we started the engines we sat down under a tree and had a sack lunch, thanking the Lord for the success so far.

After lunch we started the engines while the three Zambian helpers watched us. The mud pump was circulating the drilling fluid, so Greg began lowering the drill bit into the ground. It went smoothly for the first five feet. We added another drill stem and began lowering the drill once again. At about eight feet the circulation from the hole to the surface abruptly stopped while the pump was still supplying forty gallons per minute into the open drilled borehole. We couldn't believe our eyes. Where was this fluid going? The mud pit was almost empty of water, so we shut the unit down to try to figure out what was happening. Greg noticed that 150 feet away was a large termite mound. Sure enough, we had hit one of their underground channels that we couldn't seal up to continue drilling since the chambers below were so large in diameter and vast in number. It was a learning experience we couldn't have anticipated from any of our American drilling jobs and training. At the demonstration we would be sure to pick a site free of termite mounds.

We dismantled the equipment and loaded it into the truck to be delivered to the conference site that afternoon. Then our team left the guesthouse for the four-hour journey to Kigwa, Zambia. When we arrived, we were delighted to find comfortable accommodations and a conference ground where a well-drilling test site was available just one hundred feet from the open-air conference auditorium. That evening our team got together for prayers of thanksgiving in anticipation of what was to be a milestone event for the leadership of the Evangelical Fellowship of Zambia and Lifewater partnership.

The pastors began arriving the next day. Most traveled by bus, a few by car, and three walked several miles to the conference center from local communities. Our first official meeting would begin that evening in the outdoor conference auditorium. Joseph and Helmut used the evening for a time of praise and worship as they welcomed us and introduced the schedule for the next few days. After we were announced, we had a wonderful time sharing how the Lord had brought each of us to that place for that time and for those kingdom purposes.

Lorraine was surrounded by ladies after we closed the official first evening program. They pummeled her with questions about America, marriage and American men. Some of the questions got quite personal, but she felt comfortable answering them. The Zambian women were all smiles as they learned things totally unrelated to the training sessions we'd planned about safe water, health and hygiene.

Lorraine and I were offered a bedroom in the home of the conference grounds director. It was clean and neat. We had our own bathroom with a cold shower. A hole in the floor near the toilet was home to many frogs who emerged at night. We tiptoed around them to use the bathroom. Since the climate was quite humid, hot water was not really necessary. After a few moments one's body adapted to the water temperature. Our beds had mosquito nets but we still examined the room closely for any insects in the room. Lorraine used her trusty can of Raid in the corners and other areas where they could be hiding. We didn't need to contract malaria!

Although all of the attendees were eager to see the drilling machine demonstration, we insisted that the classroom discussions were very important to understand the overall community development process. It was especially important to learn how our efforts would provide an opportunity to present the gospel. We wanted the pastors to explain their plans for gospel outreach components for their Lifewater projects.

They assembled in the auditorium for our introductory classes. Greg led a session on groundwater and how to utilize this natural resource. He explained how so many places of the world were using hand-dug wells with ropes and buckets to access this underground water supply. He helped them understand how drilled wells were far superior to open wells for maintaining safe drinking water on a continuing basis. I was delighted to see how many were taking notes and appeared to be learning about this new subject. These instructional classes were helping them understand waterborne diseases and the damaging health results.

At the same time Lorraine was leading a session in another room on health and hygiene. She was fortunate to have several nurses and a doctor to validate what she was teaching. She'd brought several "Water for the World" documents on the subject, and these medical professionals were quite pleased at how plainly these resources had been written and printed, so that they were easy to understand. She was thrilled at the turnout and enthusiasm they had for the conference.

That afternoon she would be training her groups in soap making while

Greg and I would be demonstrating the drilling rig. It turned out many of the pastors wanted to attend both events, which we'd not anticipated. Many wanted to hear about the health and hygiene subjects, together with soap making, which were the sessions Lorraine would be teaching. As soon as some of them saw us turn on the machine and drill a few feet they were convinced they understood this process and several sneaked off to go to the soap-making session. We did not anticipate this curiosity. Since the time was short, and we didn't have time for single events, we had to run them in parallel time frames. It was necessary for us to have two events at the same time to get all of the training sessions completed within the short conference. The next day Lorraine showed the women how to remove the soap from the mold. The soap molds were lined with a pretty printed cotton cloth she'd brought from our scrap bin at home. To her surprise the ladies asked her for the scraps of cotton cloth. Though they were soaked with a caustic solution, they promised to wash them before using them. Their need and perspective on the value of what we took for granted challenged our hearts.

Lifewater volunteers have learned that, no matter how intently you plan or study the culture, you will always encounter surprises that throw your plans somewhat awry. Only the Lord puts things together and, in so doing, He receives the credit for the successful outcome. This is how it must be. At the concluding evening event we had a great time of singing, prayers and celebration for what we had all experienced in our newfound fellowship as we partnered in one effort for the gospel of Jesus Christ.

I was videotaping many of these events and interviews with pastors to document what these leaders were experiencing. They shared how they would be using their newly acquired information to bless the people in their areas. As these pastors spoke into the camera, I was almost overcome with their joyful emotion. It became hard for me to hold the camera steady as I recorded some of their excited words and gratitude for the Lifewater team visitation.

After returning from the conference, Joseph Imakando, Greg and I went shopping in Lusaka for supplies. Greg went into the grocery store and Joseph went to the hardware store, leaving me in the car. I preferred to stay there because if I went with Joseph the prices would go up. As I was sitting in the passenger side, a young man came up to my open window and told me he had a special bargain for me. As he spoke he dropped a large, rough green emerald in my hands. He walked away quickly, leaving me holding the valuable stone. In a few seconds he walked back to the car, tipping his head the other direction and told me he would sell it to me for the equivalent value of US$500.

I said, "No, thank you," and lifted it up in a gesture for him to come and pick it up.

He retreated a step or two and said, "Okay, four hundred."

I repeated, "No, thank you."

The price finally got down as low as $100. I kept refusing and suggested he pick it up. It felt like a setup. The spot where we were parked, in front of a bank, was a great place to find tourists changing their money. I wouldn't be surprised if some undercover police officers were waiting for me to make a buy, since emeralds for sale on the street are illegal. These beautiful gemstones were one of Zambia's natural resources and sales were highly regulated.

On one other occasion Martin Hamann came with me to Zambia to assist the local drilling crew with advanced training. During a visit to an established two-year old national drilling team, I was taking pictures of some of the wells they had constructed as they were being used by local people. I was in the field when we happened on a water pump being used by a couple of fragile young girls. They were loading their containers for the long walk home. I watched them pump the water into these big buckets, assuming both of them would carry the big one. But as I prepared to take a picture I was startled to see they were preparing to lift this heavy load for only one to carry. This picture will stick indelibly in my memory for the rest of my life. After I photographed the scene I watched in amazement as this young fragile girl staggered under the heavy load as she walked away from the well site. I had to set down my camera to wipe away my tears.

Two young farmer volunteers from the San Joaquin Valley of California joined me on another trip to train a group of Zambian agricultural school graduates. We were introducing the new techniques of drip irrigation systems. It was our hope that they could introduce this culturally different technique for raising a crop to a poor society of subsistence farmers. At best, subsistence farmers have severe trouble finding food if the crop fails. At worst, some starve to death. These farmers desperately needed to learn how to raise more crops on the small plots of land they were using. It would take courage on their part to try this farming technique.

Drip irrigation puts the water right where the plant needs it and does so with about half the volume used with other irrigation techniques. Lifewater was unable to pay these young Zambian agriculture students a salary for this introductory program. We were hoping they would find a sufficient subsidy from the Evangelical Fellowship of Zambia, but the Fellowship did not have sufficient funds to carry on the project. It's one of those opportunities where success could have been achieved had the resources been available. At this point in Lifewater's development, our budget didn't include sufficient funding to cover a demonstration plot in each town where these systems were being introduced. Also, to ensure success, we would have needed to supply a small salary for the development workers.

The cost for the drip system could easily have been recouped from the harvest and sale of some of the first crop. In fact, the plan was for each farmer receiving this first drip system gift to agree to purchase one for his neighbor the following year. This could have made it self-perpetuating. Lifewater was unable to fund this project sufficiently, though, to help the workers with a subsistence wage while they established the program.

CHAPTER 19
Zimbabwe: Solar Oven and Water Strategy

I received a phone call from USAID inviting Lifewater to be a part of their U.S. exhibit of technologies for agriculture that they were displaying in Bulawayo, Zimbabwe. Their invitation included all of the trip expenses except airfare. They asked what type of technology we could demonstrate at this trade fair, and I'd just designed a Fresnel lens solar cooker. The shape of the parabolic reflector was similar in optics to a frog's eye. This type of lens would be a uniquely adapted configuration that would concentrate light by a factor of four at a parallel focal point. I shaped the apparatus in two dimensions like the Fresnel lenses. I suggested that we could display this as a new technique for solar cooking and could also explain our village water well strategy for rural poor communities. USAID agreed.

We received a formal invitation and paperwork via Federal Express. We selected a twelve- by twelve-foot exhibit booth and submitted our design. The design of the full USAID fair exhibit would be an eighty-foot-diameter pie-shaped structure. Lifewater would have one of twelve pie-shaped booths. USAID arranged for it to be picked up and flown to the destination conference grounds.

I flew to New York and then took South African Airways in two twelve-hour segments to Zimbabwe. We had four days to display and a day on each end to set up and tear down our exhibits. The attendees came from all over the south of Africa. Many were very interested in our ministry and begged me to help them in their villages. I could only take down names and addresses and explained that I could not promise a project until we designed it and were able to obtain funding to implement it.

The exhibit fair opened with a flood of viewers and was overwhelming for the first few hours. USAID had told us that the first day was always the biggest. My little slide projector drew a big crowd every time I started up the show of some twenty slides. It contained scenes from Haiti and Uganda, showing the Lifewater strategy to help train and equip national crews to provide safe water in their communities. Each time the show was over, several people hung around to give me their addresses and ask for help. Sometimes the urgency in their eyes and voices took my breath away. It was difficult not to promise that Lifewater would send a team right away.

I had to explain that we were a small Christian ministry supported by friends and churches. I could only try to assuage their disappointment by saying, "We will pray; you pray; and we will see how God answers."

I remember particularly one lady's group from Botswana. I believe there were four or five of them visiting this show. They came with a specific need to develop safe water sources in their community. When they found me they were especially delighted, and we corresponded over the next year. I was disappointed to never be able to fund this project. This is another one of those incidents where delays meant that these women, and others like them, would have to endure babies dying while the wheels of progress and project planning ground on too slowly. This problem frustrated me. As hard as I tried to communicate this difficulty to major donors, foundations and civic groups, it was very seldom that I was able to get someone to act immediately with a grant.

During the second day we had a visit from Zimbabwe's president, Mr. Banana. He was very gracious to stop at each booth and wish us all well in our future connections with local people. His entourage included a dozen or more stately dressed men and women scribbling notes and taking literature from each of the exhibits. The next day Prime Minister Mugabe came by with his entourage. This time there were Marines with automatic weapons protecting him. Nobody took information or literature because they were in a hurry.

I met some people from the Blair Institute in Harare. They told me about their success with the design of a latrine privy. Lifewater then began using a modified design of that structure in our own sanitation presentations.

PART IV

Lifewater Innovations and Strategies

CHAPTER 20
Short-Term Workers

I've seen a revival among complacent Christians who have joined the ranks of current believers already expressing their faith by "word and deed." Ministries focused on training and equipping nationals to meet basic human needs in their communities exemplify this "word and deed" expression. Today, perhaps more than ever before, active Christians are showing they care about the plight of the poor around the world. As such, "word and deed" ministries like Lifewater International are challenged by the exciting task of expanding our services around the world.

In the past, we were challenged to accomplish the vision by using short-term workers (STWs) with special skills to get the job done in the shortest length of time. Here's how it worked in two different environments:

First, and most commonly, these STWs would partner with a local Christian agency that was aware of the needs in their communities but unable to fully help their own people due to their meager assets. When locals partner with workers from the developed world, they can obtain the assets they would otherwise lack. This births a team that is able to show Christian love in action. The teams working in the communities are always asked to tell what motivates them to help the poor. The STWs have the opportunity to give a statement about their own experiences with the Lord. These opportunities also allow the local Christians to present the gospel in their own language and culture.

The impact of Christians from the other side of the world joining local Christians to serve the poor is powerful. Partnerships demonstrate the Christian belief about loving one another by putting love into action. This unconditional love of God for His people regardless of race, religion, gender or status validates our faith and draws people to the Lord.

The second environment includes countries that are closed to traditional missionaries. These countries will often accept a Christian worker bringing genuine assistance in the form of training and equipment. Simply put, governments usually consider the provision of basic human needs as an acceptable reason to permit entry by foreigners. These encounters are usually a longer effort requiring multiple STW trips, but the potential for ministry is strong. Often, local residents in these countries are unacquainted with Christianity, but they are most intrigued to learn why foreigners would travel so far and invest so much just to help them. This second type of project—in traditionally closed countries—also leads to training and equipping people to become independent. Teams working in these communities are also always asked to tell what motivates them to help the community. The STWs have the opportunity to "give an answer to everyone who asks…to give the reason for the hope you have" (1 Peter 3:15).

Biblical principles of Christian living and the story of Jesus are introduced by the personal testimonies of the workers. As stated above, this type of evangelism is less threatening to governments that have developed a negative policy toward traditional Christian missionary methods. STWs are seldom considered "missionaries." Their short stay allows them to be considered community development workers.

These strategies were much more cost effective than the traditional model in which churches invested in sending career missionaries overseas to bring the gospel to unreached people groups. In the past missionaries' salaries and travel needed to be completely covered by the sending church and/or agencies. The new short-term professional Christian worker often funds much or all of his or her own costs. This frees up donors to participate by contributing to the costs of training, equipping and empowering the locals for their independence.

Lifewater International uses the simplest of all strategies to fulfill its mission and vision by providing for people's most basic physical need, safe drinking water, as well as their spiritual need for "living water" (John 4:10). On average, we provided a lifetime supply of safe water at the exceptional value of less than $5 per person. Everyone needs water to sustain physical life and living water to sustain new life into eternity. We have been blessed so that we can bless others. "A cup of cold water" is a blessing we have been given in America and one we are able to bless others with in the thirsty regions of the world (Matthew 10:42). Pastor William Ndegwa, of Kenya, testifies, "Water is life and it means so much to any living creature. Without water, there is no life, and life would be very difficult even to imagine."

The connection between caring for the physical body and ministering to the soul is eloquently defined by Pastor Samuel Yameogo of the Evangelical Churches of Burkina Faso, "If you want to preach only to our souls, go to the place of the dead. That is the place where body and soul are separate. Here on earth, to reach my soul you cannot neglect my body."

In most countries the days have passed when a missionary showed up with only a Bible in his hand. The effectiveness of today's Christian worker is vastly increased when we share the gospel and help others learn a skill that will improve the quality of daily life. Today's Christian STW needs skills to show, in tangible ways, the grace and love of the God of the Bible.

CHAPTER 21
Short-Term Worker Conferences

At one period in our history, the annual Lifewater Volunteer Conference was growing by 30 percent each year. New volunteers represented approximately one-third of the attendees. Another one-third consisted of volunteers who had been on an overseas project trip. The last group were our team leaders, professional water resource management specialists. They were dedicated Christian workers sold on the ministry of Lifewater who'd become our best skilled training personnel.

In preparation for each conference, our staff prepared a large display board that stood at the front of the room. Arranged in vertical columns, this board had sticky notes with the names of countries, types of projects and assigned team leaders.

New volunteers were given a two-hour orientation and history session to bring them up to speed on Lifewater's ministry. A time of questions and answers helped each one determine if the Lord was calling him or her to serve with Lifewater. We lost very few at this point because, before making the decision to attend the conference, they had been researching whether this kind of Christian ministry was for them. They'd already sought and received counsel from their family and Christian friends. By the time this preparatory research was completed, most who had registered had a sense of validation that the Holy Spirit was leading them. I believe these prayerful steps in preparation to come to a conference was a major reason we had very few dropouts.

The conference ran from Monday through Saturday. At the beginning of the conference, I would explain briefly all of the projects on the board. All of the information was available on the back table with details anyone could pursue in depth. A photocopier was provided so that people could make copies for their own notebooks for future reference and planning. At each conference, staff would provide a white notebook for each attendee that contained sections on the who, what, where, when and why of Lifewater. Saturday was the day of decision.

During the conferences there were also demonstrations and technical presentations. By the late 1990s the new LS 100 drilling machine was set up outside the conference room in an open grassy area where one of the team would demonstrate the operation, drilling down only about ten feet. This event would last a couple of hours, and we'd stop frequently for questions and answers.

Volunteers were gathered in "team huddles" over the final three days, organized around specific projects. These were times in which the team leader would explain the nature and scope of a specific project. To identify these team huddles, a five-foot flagpole with the country name was erected to identify the huddle. New volunteers were encouraged to circulate among the huddles and drop in on the discussions to see if there was a fit for their time frame and skills.

On Saturday I would announce: "Now I am going to ask you to take the next step in this process by becoming an active volunteer." They'd been given opportunities to read, discuss and pray about which of these potential projects looked good to them. After a few minutes of final questions and answers, I led the group in prayer, asking that the Lord would direct the steps of each volunteer being called into this ministry and into each specific project. Then I invited everybody to bring up a yellow sticky note, with his or her name on it, and place it on the board under the project they had chosen. I then invited them forward for a prayer of dedication. That simple public act was just one more step in responding to the Lord by saying, "Here am I. Send me!" (Isaiah 6:8).

Interestingly, there were about three or four occasions when someone would come to our conference who had not yet committed his or her life to Jesus Christ as Lord and Savior. They'd quickly realize, though, that this was a group of Christians who really believed in Jesus. On these occasions, one of our staff or a team leader would have the opportunity to lead this new volunteer to saving faith in Jesus Christ. Since Jesus said one soul is worth the whole world (Mark 8:36), this evangelism slice of the Lifewater ministry was no small contribution.

On each project the team leader, team members and our staff did everything humanly possible to organize each project in advance of implementation. Once all the scheduling, purchasing, equipment shipping and travel arrangements were completed, the success always depended on the Lord Himself. Zechariah learned this same lesson as God told him,

"Not by might nor by power, but by my Spirit" (Zechariah 4:6). This lesson continues to teach us that God works His will through His people. "The hands of Zerubbabel have laid the foundation of this temple; his hands will also complete it" (Zechariah 4:9). Trusting in Christ is a wonderful process of sanctification for all of us. We trust God for the outcome but continue to realize that our "hands will also complete it."

Over the years I have awakened often in the night to pray for some volunteer on the field. The Holy Spirit prodded me to use prayer as the critical support mechanism for our work when we faced difficulty and uncertainty. I'm sure other staff, board members and volunteers were doing the same. The Lifewater team runs on prayer.

Our conferences have become wonderful, exciting experiences as teams who have returned share their trips in the evenings with pictures, videos and stories of God's footprints unseen. Together we celebrated many successes that could only be attributed to the hand of the Lord.

The Lord continues to provide Lifewater with an ever-expanding pool of experienced, dedicated people. Only God knows the future contributions these teams will make to alleviate the suffering of so many poor communities struggling to survive with polluted water.

CHAPTER 22
The Bush Pump

One of the best results from a Lifewater trip was my introduction to the Zimbabwe bush pump. Though there are several other commercially manufactured hand pumps, none compare to the simplicity of the device, a pump using lever action to extract water from a borehole well. I was very impressed at how this pump had been proven to work in villages, especially how easy it was easy to maintain and repair. This impressive functionality, plus the simplicity of its design, makes it superior to any other hand pump.

The Blair Institute in Harare, Zimbabwe, designed it. I learned that some twenty thousand of these pumps had been operating in Zimbabwe over the previous twenty years. They were statistically proven to be the best design, most cost-effective and most maintainable pump of anything on the market.

I had to ask the question "Why are they not being made and used all over the world?"

The answer was simple. The commercial companies offering complicated metal pumps had connections with the governments and required their hand pumps to be the only ones authorized for sale. Nobody was helping poor villagers discover this simple design that they could make and maintain for themselves. That's just not the way the business world works. I later discovered that the average cost for a village bush pump was about $167. The average cost of commercially made hand pumps was over $500, with some as much as $1,700. How sad to ignore this great design while the profit-making enterprises continued to suppress this simple, usable pump!

Odo Siahaya, our chief engineer, and I designed and printed plans that we distributed to every requesting agency knocking on our door. Odo built several Lifewater bush pumps and began shipping them to our current projects. He took one with him to Guinea-Bissau so that the local people could begin to manufacture them for replacement hand pumps in their country. He shipped two or three to our Lifewater-Kenya team, and with Odo's supervision, they began to build them. Odo made a return trip to Kenya to help them through some troubles. The local team had been building some of these bush pumps, but their tolerances were sloppy. In the field pumps were operating only a short time and would need repairs. Odo showed them that keeping good tolerances during the construction of the parts was critical for making a good product. From then on they got it right and have been continuing to supply them for water wells.

Odo also introduced our plastic cylinder concepts, once again, and tried to help people build a cottage industry. We experimented with ideas of how to train simple village shop workers to finish them, since they needed to be drilled and tapped before these parts could be used in cylinders.

Lifewater has now introduced the bush pump successfully to several national agencies in the developing world. These pump shops are now supplying this village-level maintenance hand pump at a growing rate. Thank the Lord this is now becoming a valuable village asset. Though the water bearers still carry heavy loads back to their families, the bush pumps are still wonderful improvements.

CHAPTER 23
Pump Repair Ministry

Many poor rural communities have problems with inoperative hand pumps, sitting over valuable community water wells, when the local people have never been taught how to repair them. It didn't occur to me as a critical problem until I witnessed it in Haiti.

Moving the handle up and down, the people would say, "We used to do this and water came out of here, but now no water." Then they would ask, "Could you help us?"

It was clear to me this was an easier job, and more cost-effective, than drilling new wells. Many of these broken-down wells needed only a few dollars' worth of repairs and the expertise of a crew with equipment to repair them. I resolved to begin a new Lifewater program to repair wells with volunteers willing to be trainers in some of the most difficult areas of the world.

The first pump repair volunteer signed up at the 1997 volunteer conference. Bill Armstrong, just back from Burkina Faso, told me that he would like to return and assist folks there with their existing inoperative wells. Bill told me that the government estimated that of the forty-four thousand wells in their country, half were not working. A big job!

Bill and I had some good conversations about how to develop our strategy. As a mechanical engineer, he understood the problem and what it would take to train people. They would need to learn how to diagnose the problem and repair pumps. Bill and I put together a list of parts he would need in order to work on the first project. We agreed that the Lifewater bush pump design was something he could train his crews to build and use. Bill went to his mission agency and suggested that he could be very useful as their missionary by meeting this basic human need in conjunction with a witness to the Christian gospel. As with many mission agencies Lifewater had approached, they were reluctant to become involved and denied him funding for this project. Bill had enough money to finance himself on a shoestring budget for the first year to prove the strategy of this type of program. He was willing to set out for Burkina Faso if I'd be willing to keep him supplied to make repairs. In faith I agreed.

Still eager to secure reliable funding, I wrote a proposal to the First Fruit Foundation. Rob Martin, the foundation's executive director, invited me to visit his office to explain more about the project. First Fruit ended up sending us our first grant that funded Bill Armstrong for his initial year of training people to repair wells and pumps.

It is great to know that Burkina Faso pump repair teams are still repairing wells all over the country. Literally thousands of people are drinking safe water again. Only God knows the number of babies and people whose lives have been saved because of Bill Armstrong's willingness to help people in need. He willingly gave up a great career and salary as an engineer to become a kingdom worker.

Before constructing a new well for a village, Lifewater teams now require that it be drilled in a place where the public can freely access the water source. In the past, some wells had been completed on private land where the owner promised to always allow the public to access the water. But in a few cases, these owners put up fences with gates and locks. Not a good result!

My long-range vision for Lifewater has included setting up regional centers in seven strategic locations around the world. Six to eight national centers would surround these regional centers. Lifewater International would supply the regional centers with personnel, equipment and training facilities as well as with business and communications systems. National centers would be manned by Lifewater-trained local managers. Local supplies and expert training would improve the productivity of Lifewater training crews in a two-hundred-mile radius. I hope and pray these centers will someday exist.

CONCLUSION

My life has been shaped by many people and opportunities: my parents, my loving and wonderful wife, Lorraine, our children, more than fifty years of reading and memorizing the Word of God, my church experiences, my business experiences and the ministry of Lifewater. And throughout my days, I've noticed many "it just so happened" events, which some would label as "coincidence" but which I've recognized as God's "footprints unseen" leading me through my life. This sense of God's presence is what has given me the desire and courage to press on to the high calling of Christ until I meet my Lord in eternity.

Today the growing disparity between rich and poor seems to be widening. The Bible teaches that this gap is a result of our sin, mainly greed and selfishness. Proverbs 14:31 warns, "Whoever oppresses the poor shows contempt for their Maker, but whoever is kind to the needy honors God."

Yet Jesus taught that a Christian lifestyle would include a witness to the gospel and the kind of loving service he spoke of in Matthew 25, namely help for the poor. These two mandates of a Christian lifestyle, coupled with the modern conveniences of rapid, affordable travel and convenient communication, make the best platform for helping unreached people receive and respond to the gospel.

Jesus gave his people the ministry of reconciliation, as told in Matthew 28:18-20:

> Jesus came to them and said, "All authority in heaven and on earth has been given to me. Therefore go and make disciples of all nations, baptizing them in the name of the Father and of the Son and of the Holy Spirit, and teaching them to obey everything I have commanded you. And surely I am with you always, to the very end of the age.

And in 2 Corinthians 5:18-21, Paul echoes Jesus' exhortation.

> All this is from God, who reconciled us to himself through Christ and gave us the ministry of reconciliation: that God was reconciling the world to himself in Christ, not counting people's sins against them. And he has committed to us the message of reconciliation. We are therefore Christ's ambassadors, as though

> God were making his appeal through us. We implore you on Christ's behalf: Be reconciled to God. God made him who had no sin to be sin for us, so that in him we might become the righteousness of God.

Going into all the world to proclaim the gospel—calling men, women and children to be reconciled to God—is central to the Lord's plan for making disciples of all peoples. We go to help the poor and are prepared to share our faith. In every moment we are prepared to give the irrefutable argument of our personal testimony, "an answer to everyone who asks you to give the reason for the hope that you have" (1 Peter 3:15).

While using our experience and professional skills to bless people in need, Lifewater and other mercy and compassion ministries have experienced increasing numbers of volunteers willing to go to the places the rest of the world has forgotten. Through this strategy, we work toward reaching the nations. It will be their joy, and ours, when in heaven we hear the new song "from every tribe and language and people and nation" (Revelation 5:9). In order to bring a tangible witness for Christ in short-term missions, we must package our Christian love as solutions to basic human needs for the sake of those we serve. This is what can bridge the gap created in the absence of long-term relationships that are central to traditional mission models.

As the ministry of Lifewater continues, I pray that many who will continue to receive physical water will discover the love of the One who called himself Living Water.

APPENDIX

LIFEWATER FRIENDS AND PARTNERS

FREE METHODIST CHURCH OF MOZAMBIQUE

We were fortunate to have a request through the Free Methodist Church in America to assist their partner church the Free Methodist Church of Mozambique. Dr. Don Anderson and Randy Fain were the original Lifewater team members to train a local group from Mozambique on the LS 100 drilling machine. Randy also helped them install a solar power system they had on the site.

Several trips and a few years of training later, this team had been successful in many areas. Two years ago we had several U.S. senators pay a visit to this project in Mozambique. Two of our finest team leaders, Pat Klever and Dr. Kanan Patel Coleman, were there to escort them and answer questions. The senators were touring disadvantaged African nations impacted by the HIV/AIDS epidemic. The senators learned that safe drinking water is the most important health benefit these people can receive. They returned excited about including provision of safe water in the bill before Congress to fund this effort.

LONE STAR BITS COMPANY

Harry and about twenty-three other water resource management professionals from all over the United States and Canada came to our conference in 1989. This was the first conference where we had a full week of demonstrations, classroom lectures and water development papers presented. All of this was set within a rich time of Christian fellowship and meaningful Bible studies.

Harry's dedication and vision was essential in the development of another ministry. Harry had an opportunity to go to Peru to operate a large well-drilling machine for a mission compound. The provision of safe water was important for the mission's growth and operations. With the success of this project, and Harry's observations of the poor villages, the Holy Spirit drew him to consider full-time ministry in this field. Harry gathered some of his friends from church and formed the organization Living Water International.

Their ministry differed from Lifewater on one basic Christian principle. Living Water was responding to these agencies utilizing a Christian principle based on Jesus' story of the Good Samaritan (Luke 10:25-37). This principle of Christian service says, irrespective of how much it would cost for each project, they would attempt to provide water wells one at a time. On the other hand, Lifewater was responding to requesting agencies on the Christian principle of the good steward (Luke 12:42-28). We fielded so many requests that we were required to calculate where we would achieve the greatest number of people served for the dollars invested.

Our two ministries have partnered well through the years. Living Water's board member Larry Laird built a training facility on his ranch at Quantum Lakes, Texas. We have held multiple training sessions for our volunteers there.

LIFEWATER CANADA

I received a call in July of 1996 from Jim Gehrels in Thunder Bay, Canada. He explained that he was the director of the Water Quality Records Office for the Canadian government. He'd read a news story and wanted to know what the Lifewater International team of Christian engineers would be doing at our conference that October. He told me he was interested in coming. I explained, in brief, that we were a team of water resource management specialists using our skills and experience to help the rural poor develop and maintain safe drinking water supplies in Jesus' name.

He answered, "Great!"

So I queried, "Are you a Christian?" This is a question I always asked people like Jim who are calling me for the first time to find out what Lifewater is all about.

Jim replied, "Yes, I am a Christian and I agree with your objectives. I have another Christian friend who's a fireman, Glenn Stronks, who would also like to attend this conference."

I sent them the Lifewater volunteer applications, together with two invitations for the conference. Jim and Glenn showed up along with about thirty other like-minded people. Twenty of them were first-timers!

Per usual, the following year's projects were displayed on the large display board. One I almost excluded, due to the danger of rebels. It was a project in Liberia. As with all projects, we had prepared a blue binder with the details provided to us by the requesting agency. I put the Liberia sticky note on the board along with all the others. I noticed that Jim and Glenn moved around from one project huddle possibility to another during the conference. But they kept coming back to the Liberia folder.

When I announced it was the time of decision, Jim came up and said, "I know you have moved Liberia off the board of likely projects for 1997." Then he said, "Bill, I feel called to Liberia."

My knees got weak as I looked him in the eye and said, "I'm sure you've read the details and the possible dangers you will face. Are you sure?"

At this point I felt like I had made an error by having brought the Liberia details to the conference. There were more than enough projects where we would be safe and welcome. On the other hand, I knew the Lord would not have us step back from trouble. Christians of the past faced worse conditions! However, making decisions for people's involvement far from home was a real dilemma for me. The responsibility I'd shoulder for allowing this project to come to the board was a large step of faith that would set a precedent for the future by impacting Lifewater policies.

I told Jim and Glenn I was feeling led by the Spirit to give approval but would consult with the board of directors for a final word. I felt confident they would give their permission. Jim and Glenn began planning the trip.

As I was praying in my room before the banquet, where all of the volunteers and their assignments would be announced, the Holy Spirit reconfirmed Jim's decision. He was being guided to do the project and I should validate his decision and continue to trust the Lord for positive indicators. The tension in my soul eased a bit; however, this was to be a learning experience for me as the founder and director of Lifewater. Having the gift of administration meant I needed to be willing to own the decisions we made.

Jim's leadership on the Liberia project was outstanding.

FRIENDS WHO INFLUENCED MY LIFE

DON HAMILTON

One Sunday in the 1970s I met Don Hamilton at Bethany Church. He was a Bible scholar and taught our adult Sunday school class. Don was a brilliant engineer. At the time he was heading up a department at Electo-Optical Systems. He served in the facsimile research division located in Pasadena. They were working on a new invention called "fax machines." Don told us the company was predicting access to fax machines in every shopping center and industrial park. They thought that was a bold prediction.

Don had used crutches to walk since polio had made his legs atrophy in childhood. But his mind was very sharp and he excelled at managing things. He was also a great pianist. His communication skills exceeded those of most of his peers. Don taught me how to create a business plan using measurable, achievable goals. We began a project together and started with all the assumptions of the business concepts.

GRAHAM PATTERSON

Graham was an ex-army major and a fine Christian gentleman ten years my senior who had a successful earth-moving contracting business. He was an elder in our church who I looked up to for spiritual counsel and friendship. He was one of the men who I would join in the sanctuary prayer room before the morning and evening services. For a few moments we shared concerns and then prayed that our pastor's message would be clear and that the Holy Spirit would draw people to respond to the gospel. Graham became one of Lifewater's first members on our board of directors. He and his wife, Alice, gave generously over the first few years to help us with our early expenses. Graham was one of my enthusiastic supporters, often saying, "I think you're on the right track, Bill."

ODO SIAHAYA

I met Odo Siahaya at the first Christian Technical & Engineering Ministries conference I organized at the William Carey International University in Pasadena. He came there as a representative of the relief and development arm of Mission Aviation Fellowship. At this conference he came to see the Stover S300 rig we'd recently purchased for them that was to go to Indonesia.

Odo became my right-hand man. He and his wife, Beverly, had overseas missionary experience and helped me learn a considerable amount about the lifestyle of missionaries. Odo was always helpful in constructing things and preparing for our annual Lifewater volunteer conferences. His personal skills and assets included engineering and design insights, a dry sense of humor, a humble demeanor and a fine Christian lifestyle. He has been, and always will be, one of the persons I respect most. He was one of the important people contributing to the development of the Lifewater ministry.

Odo had a way of convincing me to try a slightly different design or modification to something we were inventing for "village-level maintenance." Village-level maintenance was the major objective of any agency attempting to help the rural poor with sustainable projects. If it was too complicated, or relied on parts that were only commercially attainable, the project would not be something that poor rural communities could maintain. I designed a cylinder valve cage that could be molded out of very durable plastic to replace a very expensive bronze-machined part. The question we had to ask was "Can we make hand-operated tools for the rural poor so that they can learn to perform the precision threading required to produce a cage accurately?" Odo and I struggled with these parts and techniques in our shop until we had the tools and parts that a mechanically minded young person in the villages could learn to use.

JEFF AND SHARON BJORCK

One Sunday in church Lorraine and I turned around in our chairs to greet Jeff and Sharon Bjorck. It was their first visit to Christ Community Church, where my son Donald was the senior pastor. We introduced ourselves and struck up a conversation. Jeff was a new Fuller Seminary professor in the School of Psychology. He and Sharon were very interested in the Christ Community Church statement of faith.

I did the best I could with brief answers amid the noisy chattering of people fellowshipping after church. I suggested calling him later in the afternoon to try to answer the questions more fully. That phone call lasted a half an hour or more. Jeff really put me to the test of what I believed and what I understood about the church's statement of faith. Because he and Sharon came back the next Sunday, I assumed they felt it was compatible with their theology.

Jeff, who became a close friend and prayer partner, was a gift from the Lord. These special times with Jeff were especially encouraging to me as he would counsel me and pray for my unusual workload with the Lifewater ministry. We were going through so many expansion growth pains that I was under stress and needed the Lord's strength to carry on. In 1999 I submitted Jeff's name to the Lifewater board of directors as a possible candidate. After an interview, he was received by a unanimous vote.

Throughout our acquaintance, Jeff has been a strong encourager for me, consistently offering wise counsel from a practical and Christian perspective. This became especially true during 1997 when I announced my intended retirement to the board.

HANK BODA

Hank was the development director for Azusa Pacific College. Because of his experience as an attorney, he was skillful in raising funds from major donors. His winsome Christian way usually persuaded people of wealth to make sizable grants to the college. He was also great counsel for me during that time between 1995 and 1999 when Lifewater finally hired the new executive director, Dan Stevens. I was struggling with some important decisions through this period of time, balancing the management of the ministry and the need for adding personnel to meet the growing demands for the services of Lifewater overseas. Hank always had good advice and would offer a prayer to back it up. We always agreed it was best to leave it in the Lord's hands for the best answers and results.

C. DAVIS WEYERHAEUSER

We sent letters of requests to countless foundations, asking them if they would consider supporting the Lifewater ministry. One who did respond was Mr. C. Davis Weyerhaeuser, of the Stewardship Foundation in Tacoma, Washington. I thank the Lord he read my letter personally and encouraged me not to begin another Christian ministry. He thought I should join one already doing projects like ours.

I wrote back to Mr. Weyerhaeuser and told him how I had approached World Vision, Food for the Hungry, World Concern and maybe a few more. The result of these meetings and phone calls was always pretty much the same: They wished me well but did not see the need to work with a subcontracting ministry in place of having their own in-house "water expert" to manage the requests they received from the field. Some gently let me know we were considered a "wildcat" organization, too new at the game for them to seriously consider our strategy. After a few years of ministry, many of these organizations began to notice our successes. In the meantime, we were receiving dozens of requests to help Christians overseas directly.

Water resource development isn't easy. Too many mission agencies attempted to meet these needs with a "water expert" from within their agency, who often knew just enough about water resource development to be dangerous. Such projects would result in minimal success at best and failure at worst. That's why the poor rural areas of the world are littered with projects started with good intentions. So many proved to be counterproductive because the "helpers" didn't help the people learn how to sustain them.

I explained our strategy to C. Davis. Lifewater was developing a broad range of Christian water resource management specialists in many fields. They were people called to use their skill and experience in the kingdom. These "word and deed" projects were so important in fulfilling the words of Jesus and the writings of the New Testament about helping the poor. Meeting the needs of those who struggled to survive was the most important place to serve.

I was delighted to receive his second letter. He wrote that he could understand my dilemma and wished to help support the objectives and mission statement of Lifewater. I submitted a brief request and soon thereafter we received a check for $15,000.

After our first successful well-drilling project in Haiti, I hand-carried the report to George Kovats at the Stewardship Foundation. To my surprise Mr. Weyerhauser was available and decided to go to lunch with us. I'm sure George had filled him in about how we'd spent their money and suggested he take this opportunity to meet me and ask questions to determine his opinion of this investment. Over lunch he asked me many probing questions in a soft-spoken gentle way, which gave me the freedom to give full and complete answers. I explained the success of providing a lifetime supply of safe water from the wells we were drilling in Haiti for just $3.60 per person.

He was impressed with this return on investment as well as our training of nationals who would continue to impact their communities for years to come. I had to explain to him that there were several barriers to overcome, the most important one being developing cross-cultural relationships. These skills are critical to properly train rural poor people.

After we finished our lunch and conversation, C. Davis gave me a very positive send-off and confirmed that he was pleased to be the first foundation to make an investment with Lifewater. He had been instrumental in our belief that we were on the right track with this ministry of "word and deed" projects.

Thank you, C. Davis, for your Spirit-inspired encouragement that gave me a reason to persevere with the ministry of Lifewater.

ROB MARTIN

I visited First Fruit Foundation after completing the first project they funded for us in Kenya. Rob Martin probed deeply about what we were accomplishing there. I remember the way he encouraged me to keep on developing our mission policy and strategy.

Several years into our relationship, Rob came to visit me at the Lifewater facility in Irwindale. On that visit we were able to share the wonderful successes that had just been achieved by Bill Armstrong in Burkina Faso. First Fruit Foundation had given us a small grant for this first major pump repair project, and we had supplied Bill with $3,000 to repair as many wells as possible. Nine months later he sent back a report with pictures of ten wells in before and after states. He was able to repair these ten wells for approximately $300 each. These wells had all been inoperative for six months or longer, since the people didn't understand how to repair them. Bill Armstrong came along with the tools, training classroom studies and field demonstrations that helped them become sufficiently skilled to repair wells on their own. Some even remarked, "I wish we knew how easy this was years ago."

First Fruit was extremely impressed by the value: $300 to supply an average community of six hundred people with safe water again. It turns out the Lifewater pump repair program is one of the finest returns on investment I have ever found in any relief and development agency. This rate of providing safe drinking water for only $.50 per person just can't be beat. Bill Armstrong went on to produce a co-op warehouse whereby dozens of repair teams could obtain parts and supplies to keep them their schedule of repairing wells running efficiently. It seems there is no end to the need. Most local communities now consider it a bargain to have these repair teams come out and fix their wells for the cost it takes to adequately cover the expenses.

ROD THOMPSON

Lorraine and I were asked to give a short presentation about the Lifewater ministry during a dinner meeting in the fellowship hall of the First Presbyterian Church of Santa Paula, where we were new members. I made some brief introductory remarks and then we showed the twelve-minute Lifewater video.

After the dinner was over, people remained for fellowship. Rod Thompson came up to me with a big smile and said, "You are an answer to my prayers!"

I asked, "How's that?"

He explained to me how he had worked with his father as a well driller before becoming a Ventura County sheriff. Rod had been with the sheriff's department for twenty-five years and was planning to retire in 2004. He explained how he'd been asking the Lord for some way to use his skills in Christian ministry when he retired. That evening, Rod received confirmation from the Holy Spirit that this was the answer to his prayers. Beside his water well experiences, Rod brought several special skills to Lifewater. He was especially mechanically capable. Also, his training as a police officer provided keen negotiating skills in difficult conditions. He has since been involved in projects in Haiti and China and recently he became the team leader for a project in Sierra Leone. He also helped develop a cottage industry for constructing single-family slow sand filters.

When Lorraine and I joined the First Presbyterian Church of Santa Paula after moving to the more rural community, I found opportunities to make some new friends. The men's fellowship at church, led by Bob Dyer, turned out to be a great bunch of guys, mostly retired like me. We met at eleven in the morning, and at noon we went to lunch together. During our hour-long meeting we had a devotion, applying biblical principles from the Scriptures. About a dozen of us from the group of twenty alternated between eating at two restaurants for lunch. The waitresses knew we were coming and took good care of us.

MICHAEL TURVEY

One afternoon I received a call from Michael Turvey at the Environmental Protection Agency office in Kansas City. He'd read about Lifewater in *U.S. Water News* and wanted to know more about it. His call came at an opportune time since we were having a conference a few weeks later. I sent him the registration information the next day. A short while later I received his application to become a volunteer and attend the conference. Mike has become our most valued team leader in Haiti. He has been there many times, taking new volunteers and introducing them to the LS 100 drilling machine and the Lifewater strategy. Mike's spiritual depth and winsome personality has made him a special friend of mine.

DR. MICHAEL CAMPANA

Dr. Michael Campana called me inquiring about the Lifewater conference. He also had read about us in U.S. Water News. He decided to come see what it was all about. I was deeply challenged by his intellect and desire to help the poorest of the poor. During the conference he was designated as the team leader for a trip to Panama. His team carried all of the parts to the LS 100 drilling rig on the first trip and returned the second time to help them with advanced training. It was a difficult project, hauling all of the equipment to a remote site in dugout canoes.

BILLY GRAHAM

And finally, I am grateful for Billy Graham, whose preaching and sermon pamphlets have challenged me to live for Christ and serve others in the only cause that matters.